The Living Chesapeake

The Living Chesapeake

J. R. SCHUBEL

The Johns Hopkins University Press

BALTIMORE AND

LONDON

Copyright © 1981 by The Johns Hopkins University Press
All rights reserved
Printed in the United States of America

The Johns Hopkins University Press, Baltimore, Maryland 21218
The Johns Hopkins Press Ltd., London

Originally published, 1981
Second printing, 1981
Third printing, 1982

Library of Congress Cataloging in Publication Data
Schubel, J. R.
  The living Chesapeake.
    1. Oceanography—Chesapeake Bay (Md. and Va.)
I. Title
GC511.S37   551.46'147   81–7286
ISBN 0–8018–2547–4   AACR2

To
Margaret, Susan, and Kathryn
and
my parents

Contents

Preface

This book is a collection of essays and photographs. The photographs were taken between 1964 and 1974 while I was on the scientific staff of The Johns Hopkins University's Chesapeake Bay Institute. The text was written in 1980.

Each chapter is an essay—an interpretive composition dealing with its subject from a personal point of view. Each is intended to stand alone. In the aggregate, they are not intended to present a comprehensive description of all the important features of the Chesapeake Bay, only a few of those that I have found particularly fascinating.

I am indebted to Dr. Donald W. Pritchard, who taught me more about the Bay than anyone, so that I might have something worthwhile scientifically to say. He also reviewed the manuscript and made numerous valuable suggestions. Without Dr. Blair Kinsman's help, however, I never would have attempted to say anything about the Bay in a non-technical way. He convinced me that I could, insisted that I do so, and showed me how. He has been a constant source of help and encouragement not only during the preparation of this book, but throughout my career. My father-in-law, Dr. M. Stewart Hostetler, read the several drafts, gave valuable editorial advice, and drew the sketch of sea level.

Without the understanding and patience of Captains David Booth, William Harris, Norman Gilbert, and, particularly, Wallace Gilbert and Charles Wessels, most of the photographs could not have been taken. To catch the best light, our days often began earlier and ended later than was necessary for science alone. William Cronin accompanied me on most of my cruises and was a constant source of inspiration and encouragement.

My assistant, Jeri Schoof, is so effective in doing her work at the Marine Sciences Research Center that mine is relatively easy. Her encouragement and dedication have been exceedingly important. The several drafts of the text were typed by C. Hof, M. Ludkewycz, and S. Risoli. Marie Eisel drew the map.

I thank Susan Bishop, Nancy Essig, Jack Goellner, James Johnston, Linda Vlasak, and Wendy Harris of The Johns Hopkins University Press for their patience, encouragement, and constructive suggestions.

Finally, I owe my greatest thanks to my wife, Margaret. She has never complained about my long and frequent absences over the years and has assumed far more than her fair share of responsibilities so that I could pursue my vocation and my avocation. She has been my most constructive and insightful critic, and she has the disagreeable habit of usually being right. She read and improved each draft. She also drew the sketches of the animals. Without her encouragement, devotion, and steadfast faith this book would not have been possible.

Publication of the book was supported, in part, by a grant to the author from the Rockefeller Foundation. I express my appreciation to Drs. Ralph Richardson and Gary Toenniessen.

The Living Chesapeake

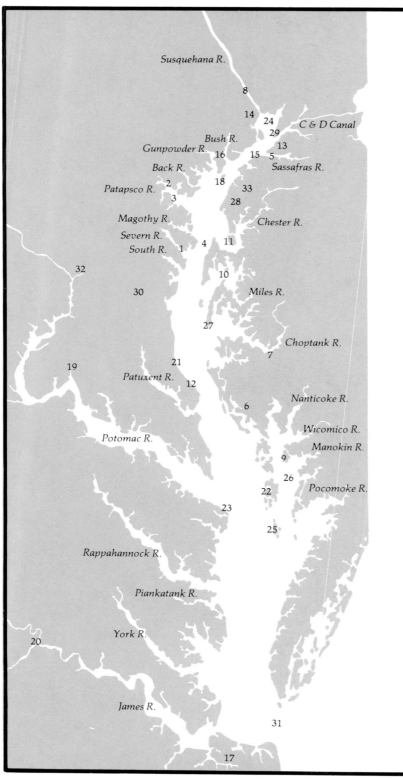

The Chesapeake Bay

1 Annapolis
2 Baltimore
3 Baltimore Harbor
4 Bay Bridge at Annapolis
5 Betterton
6 Blackwater National
  Wildlife Preserve
7 Cambridge
8 Conowingo
9 Deal Island
10 Eastern Bay
11 Eastern Neck
   National Wildlife Refuge
12 Flag Ponds
13 Grove Point
14 Havre de Grace
15 Howell Point
16 Joppatowne
17 Norfolk
18 Pooles Island
19 Port Tobacco
20 Richmond
21 Scientists' Cliffs
22 Smith Island
23 Smith Point (Potomac)
24 Susquehanna Flats
25 Tangier Island
26 Tangier Sound
27 Tilghman Island
28 Tolchester
29 Turkey Point
30 Upper Marlboro
31 Virginia Capes
32 Washington, D.C.
33 Worton Creek

20,000 years ago: There was no Chesapeake Bay. There had been one 100,000 years before, and there would be one again, but it would be another 15,000 years before a waterman could find in it his familiar landmarks. A subarctic climate gripped what would become Maryland, Delaware, and Virginia. Winters were long, harsh, and wet; summers short and cool. The mean annual temperature was 20°F colder than it is today. Where the Bay now stands the Susquehanna River flowed through a broad valley, out across a high and dry continental shelf for more than a hundred miles before it finally reached the sea. The Potomac and the Patuxent, the Choptank and the Chester, the Rappahannock, York, and Severn—all of the rivers that now enter the Bay with the exception of the James—paid tribute to the mighty Susquehanna. Even 20,000 years ago, it appears that Virginia went its own way, and the James flowed separately to the sea.

20,000 years ago: Sea level had been falling for most of the past 100,000 years. Air masses laden with moisture from the warmer oceans were chilled as they spread over the colder continents, and the moisture was wrung out of them to fall on the land as snow. At today's temperatures, moisture evaporated from the ocean and precipitated on land runs back to the ocean with little delay to complete the hydrologic cycle. This was not the case for most of the past million years and probably much longer. Through the long, frigid winters, the snow piled up deeper and deeper on the land. Some melted every summer and returned to the sea, but less than had been added the winter before. The sea continued to fall. As the snow accumulated, it slowly changed to ice as the weight of the increasing pack bore down on it. Year by year, for the better part of 100,000 years, the ice sheet had grown and thickened. Long ago the pressure had become so great that the ice sheet began to flow and spread like a plastic.

20,000 years ago: The North American ice sheet extended from the Arctic Circle all the way down into the headwaters of the Susquehanna in New

Beginnings

There rolls the deep where grew the tree.
  Oh Earth, what changes has thou seen!
There where the long street roars, hath been
  The stillness of the central sea!
—Tennyson, *In Memoriam*

3

York and Pennsylvania, averaging more than a mile in thickness. The area that was to become Maryland, Delaware, and Virginia was free of glacial ice, but not of its effects.

As the water that would otherwise have been in the ocean was locked up in the continental ice sheets, sea level fell and the shoreline retreated from the land.

20,000 years ago: Sea level was 325 feet below its present position, and the sea had pulled back completely into its own oceanic basin. Bordering it was a high and dry continental shelf which, off the middle Atlantic States, is broad and very flat, flatter than a championship billiard table. For tournament play, Willie Mosconi and Minnesota Fats will accept a billiard table which is at most 7 minutes of arc off the horizontal. The continental shelf is "flatter" than that, with a slope of only 2 minutes, dipping seaward less than four feet in every nautical mile. Were you to stand on the continental shelf, you would never be sure of reaching the sea by going "downhill."

20,000 years ago: Lush vegetation covered this sandy plain. Meadows, fresh water marsh grasses, and climax forests of boreal conifers, hemlock, and northern hardwoods flourished—trees that today are abundant only in much higher latitudes. The vegetation was luxuriant. It had to be to support the large herbivores that roamed the shelf. Ancient elephants—mammoths and mastodons—bison, musk oxen, horses, and tapir ranged over a region that in only a few thousand years would be submerged deep beneath the Atlantic Ocean. Fossil elephant bones and teeth, dredged from the continental shelf between Georges Bank and the Chesapeake Bay, are today the only reminders that these great beasts once trod through forests and meadows where fish now swim. Man had not yet arrived in this region, but he would come soon to hunt and to fish. Stream valleys deeply dissected the rolling hills of the Eastern shore and the Susquehanna had finished carving the basin that was to contain the Chesapeake Bay. 20,000 years ago. The scene was set for a change.

18,000 years ago: The climate was warmer. The mean annual temperature had been rising. The ice sheets were losing more to meltwater than they were gaining from fresh snow, and their long retreat had begun. Meltwater ran from the toe of the glacier; first in countless rivulets, then in larger streams, and, finally, into the mighty Susquehanna that raced to the sea. The sea, getting back its own, responded; it began to rise.

15,000 years ago: The sea had climbed out of its oceanic basin and had begun its relentless march across the continental shelf to reclaim its territory from mastodons and conifers, to return it to fish and plankton. The march would not stop until our present shores had been reached and perhaps not even then. "All streams run to the sea, but the sea is not full" (Ecclesiastes 1:7) did not apply in this case. The streams ran to the sea all right, but this time the sea was not only full, it was overflowing. Geologists call such oceanic attacks on the land "transgressions," as though to suggest that the sea has an obligation to stay within its own oceanic basin—a place where it has stayed for nearly 90 percent of the time over the past several million years.

The rates of vertical rise and lateral advance of the sea were dramatic, not just by geological standards, but to human perception as well.

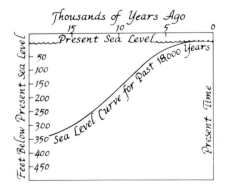

From 15,000 years ago until 5,000 years ago, the sea rose more than three feet each century. For every foot it rose, it advanced laterally across the continental shelf 1,700 feet; a rate of 50 feet a year. Waterfront property would have been an even more perilous investment 15,000 years ago than today. If your camp was not shorefront, it soon would be—just before it was drowned. For most of the past 15,000 years man has been fleeing from the sea. He still is.

The transgressing sea moved first up the valley incised into the continental shelf by the Susquehanna, pushing back the reluctant river as it came. The river was forced to retreat toward the land, and its fresh water had to move up and over the encroaching sea water. Soon the sea filled the valley, then spilled out over its steep walls and flowed out onto the gentle plain.

10,000 years ago: The advancing sea reached the present mouth of the Chesapeake Bay. The sea continued to rise, penetrating ever farther into the basin of the Susquehanna and its tributaries. The head of the Bay crept further and further inland: 8,000 years ago, the head of the Bay had reached Smith Island; 5,000 years ago, Annapolis; 3,000 years ago, Betterton at the mouth of the Sassafras. Then the rate of rise of sea level slowed appreciably, and the shoaling of the bottom by sedimentation came nearly into balance with the rise of the sea.

3,000 years ago: The Chesapeake Bay was nearly complete; it had stopped growing. Dotted with islands, tall trees extending to its shoreline, its drainage basin covered with lush vegetation, its tributaries free of fine sediments, clear, and deep. Never again would the modern Chesapeake Bay be as grand as at that moment.

3,000 years ago: The scene was set once again for a change. The Bay, barely completed, already felt the natural forces that would one day destroy it.

And so a beginning. Our Bay began 20,000 years ago, when the Susquehanna River finished carving the valley that the Bay would one day occupy. Or it began 15,000 years ago, when the ice sheets started their long retreat and the sea climbed out of its basin and headed across the continental shelf. Or it began 10,000 years ago, when the rising sea first penetrated into the Bay basin, or perhaps it began 3,000 years ago, when the head of the Bay reached its present position and a balance was struck between sedimentation and the rising of the sea. Each is only one beginning of many. Estuaries come and go with the ebb and flow of the ice ages and for each there is a beginning—and an end.

There have been other beginnings and endings; beginnings and endings of other Chesapeake Bays. To understand our own Bay, we must understand its ancestral bays—their birth, development, and death; the frequency of their comings and goings.

Ancestral bays and what they tell us about the future

To one who thoughtfully ponders the centuries and surveys the whole in the clear light of the spirit; oceans and continents alone are of account.
—Goethe, *Faust*

Each of us lives within a small segment of space-time—that part within the reach of one's senses and within the scope of one's own memories. This limitation yields a peculiarly parochial view of the world that we define, almost without thinking, as "the normal," "the usual," or "the average." The broad expanse of Chesapeake Bay is perceived as a permanent, natural feature of our Earth. There it is. It has always been there and always will be, "as it was in the beginning . . ."

One of the services of science is to create an artificial "memory," one that encompasses stretches of time far longer than those possible to individuals, to societies, or even to cultures. Only in this way can we begin to see the world as Nature sees it, on a geological time scale. From this vantage point, the familiar, "normal" world becomes a very peculiar place. Permanence becomes transience; the normal, the exception. For example, how far back in time must we go before we encounter a climate like our own? A hundred years? A thousand years? A hundred thousand years? How far back?

For the geologist, the most recent chapter in the history of the Earth occupies the last several million years. It is called the Pleistocene and it is marked by alternating glacial and interglacial episodes. In the northern hemisphere, the great continental ice sheets have waxed and waned as the world temperature has fallen and risen. The level of the sea has also risen and fallen with the retreats and advances of the great continental ice sheets. Rapid rises and falls of more than 300 feet have been common, and "Chesapeake Bays" have appeared and disappeared with each swing of the cycle.

A whole succession of "Chesapeake Bays" have been born, have matured, and have died as the sea has advanced and retreated in response to the changes in climate that caused the alternation of interglacial and glacial episodes. Each time the sea rose, a "bay" marched ahead of it across the continental shelf. If the rise was high enough, the "bay" reached well up on the continental block; even to the position of our present Bay. But not every rise was great enough to advance its "bay" so far. Many "bays" never passed the midpoint of the continental shelf. Each time the sea fell, the "bay" followed it on its retreat, lagging slightly behind as if to protest. If the sea fell so low that it dropped off the edge of the continental shelf, the attendant "bay" vanished and a new "bay" was born on the next rise. This disappearance and re-emergence of the "bay" has happened over and over during the several million years of the Pleistocene epoch.

To understand our own Bay we must go back 125,000 years to our most recent climatic analog. It was the Eemian Interglacial, a period of warm ice-free conditions similar to the present Holocene Interglacial. Sea level stood close to its present position. There was a "Chesapeake Bay" then, probably one as large and as complex as our own Bay. But it was quite different in shape and probably in location as well. To sail it, today's charts would have been useless.

The Eemian Interglacial would not last long. Its warmest period lasted but a brief 10,000 years and was followed by the abrupt onset of a cold glacial period. From 115,000 years ago to 20,000 years ago—the most recent glacial maximum—temperatures swung erratically up and down but, on the whole, dropped more than they rose. The climate deteriorated. Glaciers advanced and retreated, but gained more than they lost. The sea fell and rose in response. The "Bay" shuffled back and forth across the shelf; sometimes advancing, sometimes retreating, but generally losing ground, and finally falling into the sea only to be reborn a long time later.

Geologists use the present as a key to understanding the past. This, the principle of uniformitarianism, is a powerful tool for unraveling what has come before. But the present is a less reliable guide as to what is still to come. The perspective it offers is too limited. To clear our vision of the future, we need the higher vantage point and the longer perspective gained from an understanding of the past as well. What *has been* is a better guide to what *will be* than a knowledge of what *is* by itself. To look toward the future we must, like Janus, look toward the past at the same time.

Our Holocene Interglacial period has now lasted nearly 20,000 years. This is longer than man has lived in the middle Atlantic region, and 10,000 years longer than our Chesapeake Bay has existed.

For our private individual perceptions of space and time, 10,000 years might just as well be an eternity. It is this felt eternity that warps our judgment of the Bay's permanence and its importance in the general scheme of nature, in the evolution and survival of species, and in its critical role in the maintenance of the marine ecosystem. But nature measures time with a different clock; not with one that measures in seconds, minutes, and hours, nor even in decades, centuries, or millennia, but one that measures in tens, hundreds, thousands, and tens of thousands of millennia. Previous interglacials lasted about 10,000 years each. Our Holocene has already lasted much longer than that—twice as long. Interglacials like the Holocene, with temperatures as warm or warmer than today's, have endured for less than 10 percent of the time over the past several million years, the Pleistocene. They have occurred roughly only once in every 100,000 years and each has lasted about 10,000 years. "Chesapeake Bays" have had the same rhythm of occurrence and duration. What does the future hold for our present Bay?

An estimated 900 million cubic feet of glacial ice now covers about 10 percent of the land surface of the Earth. This ice is concentrated in the Greenland ice sheet, in the Antarctic ice sheet, and in small glaciers in the Arctic and in the Alps. Nearly 90 percent is contained in the huge Antarctic ice sheet, centered roughly on the South Pole. If this ice sheet were to melt entirely, sea level would rise nearly 200 feet. The Bay would be united with its neighbors: with the Delaware Bay, the Hudson River estuary, and Long Island Sound to the north, and with Albemarle and Pamlico Sounds to the south.

New York, Philadelphia, Baltimore, Washington, and Richmond would be submerged. But don't rush to unload your present waterfront property that would become submerged, or to invest in land in the Piedmont that would become waterfront! To melt the entire Antarctic ice cap would require thousands of years. However, partial melting could cause appreciable changes in sea level in a much shorter time.

Substantial world-wide changes of sea level within a few decades could occur only if large quantities of glacial ice were calved—split off—from the Antarctic ice sheet into the Southern Ocean. A large surge of ice from Wilkes Land could raise sea level by 50 feet in less than a century. Longer-term changes, either up or down, over thousands of years are certain. But which way will it go? Man has changed the Earth's climate. On that there is general agreement. But there all agreement ends. Some hold that the change is minor; others that the change will soon be seen to be disastrous. Some say that man is raising the temperature; others, that he is lowering it. Whether we should prepare to escape a flood or to claim newly revealed land depends upon whose predictions we trust.

In addition to worldwide changes in sea level, there are local changes because the land itself sinks under the burden of the overlying water. The land beneath and contiguous to the Chesapeake Bay is subsiding about an inch each decade. Naturally, this appears to us as a rise in sea level.

Even a relatively minor change in sea level will drastically change the Bay, and the uses we make of it. A drop in sea level of a mere 30 feet would lay bare more than 75 percent of the Chesapeake Bay; most of its oyster and clam bars would be left high and dry, its shipping channels reduced to depths of only a few feet. A small change in the other direction would be equally disastrous. A rise of only 30 feet would inundate Baltimore, Washington, Norfolk, Annapolis, and most of the Eastern Shore. The Bay would be rejuvenated, its life prolonged. Which way will sea level swing next? Up or down? The future trend of worldwide sea level changes is unclear. But change is the order of nature, and any change is almost certain to be unfortunate for man.

Even if sea level remains at its present position, the sea and the rivers that enter it will continue to battle for dominion over the valley now occupied by the Chesapeake Bay.

From the moment the sea came back to the Bay, river and sea instantly locked in combat for possession, setting off a struggle that has endured without the briefest truce for 10,000 years and that will continue until the death of this Chesapeake Bay thousands of years from now. The river constantly battles to regain its lost territory, or at least to stop the sea's assault; the sea to retain the territory it has so recently captured, and to add new lands to its growing empire. The sea has proven to be a far more persistent and tenacious enemy for the Susquehanna than the soft coastal plain sediments the river eroded to produce its expansive valley. Then the river had done its work too well, and now it must pay the price. If only the valley were not so large, the sea would not be such a formidable foe. As it is, the sea will remain in the Bay basin long after it has been expelled from most of the other coastal basins that dot the east and Gulf coasts of the United States.

When the sea invaded the Bay valley 10,000 years ago, it triggered a series of basic and fundamental changes to the water body that makes its home within this basin, changes that made it neither river nor sea. The changes started at the mouth and were transmitted progressively up the main stem of the Bay and off into each of its tributaries as the sea rose and penetrated further and further into the old river valley system. The Susquehanna struggled to push the sea back out of this valley, to retain the domain, but the task was too much even for the mighty Susquehanna. It carried more water than it had when it was master of its valley, but now things were different. The stronger the Susquehanna flowed and the harder it pushed, the more the sea rose and the farther it advanced. The assault and the retreat went on inexorably.

For now the Susquehanna would have to flow up and over the denser sea water to reach the open sea. The Patuxent and the Potomac, the Rappahannock and the York, the Choptank and the Chester, and all the other rivers that once paid tribute to the Susquehanna, now shifted their allegiance to the sea. Even the once proud

The struggle

I have seen the hungry ocean gain
  Advantage on the kingdom of the shore,
And the firm soil win of the watery main,
  Increasing store with loss, and loss with store; . . .
  —Shakespeare, *Sonnet 64*

and independent James had been captured; the sea had succeeded where the Susquehanna had failed.

Where the Susquehanna had once flowed constantly to the sea, now was a great bay, a bay whose surface rose and fell rhythmically twice each day, like a giant organism inhaling and exhaling. The bay seemed almost alive, and indeed it was. It teemed with life; life far more abundant and diverse than it had known before. The water no longer flowed constantly to the sea; its principal motion was now an oscillatory one. The Indians called it a river that flowed in two directions. But it is more than a river, more even than a river that flows in two directions—more than a tidal river—it is a giant mixing basin for sea water and fresh water. It is an estuary; the great Chesapeake Bay estuarine system; perhaps the world's most magnificent estuary.

To understand the struggle between river and sea, we must look at the details of the action. The river flows in one direction, seaward, and its water is fresh. The minuscule amounts of salts dissolved in it have been leached from the land through which it flows, and their proportions are quite different from those of the "salt" sea. Fresh water is lighter than salt water. The salinity of water is in fact a rough guide to its density; the more salt it contains, the heavier it is.

The river must get its water to the sea. There is nothing else it can do with it. More is coming all the time. Water doesn't "stack" very well, and the river has no place to store it. The river relieves itself in the only way it can. The lighter fresh water overruns the heavier salt water and flows from the Bay to the ocean in an upper layer across a lower layer of sea water. But a number of things happen to it along the way.

One of the most potent weapons in the arsenal of the sea is the tide. Were the Bay an enclosed lake, the tides would be very small; perhaps an inch or so. As it is, open to the sea at the Virginia Capes, twice each day an oceanic high tide of considerable size is delivered at its mouth by the moon and the sun which then continue on about their business. Left to its own devices the mound of water enters the Bay and rolls up its length as a free wave. The surface of the Bay rises and falls twice each day as though it were breathing. Accompanying the succession of high and low waters are tidal currents that change direction every six hours. Unlike the river, the Bay, under the governance of the sea, flows alternately in two directions; landward, then seaward, then landward again.

However, the power of the tide in the battle between river and sea is its power to mix. It is the egg beater that stirs up the water in the Bay. Were there no tide, a heavy torpid layer of salty water would lie in the bottom of the Bay and over it a lighter layer of essentially fresh water would run to the sea. Because water has some internal friction, some viscosity, though not much, some sea salt would be mixed into the upper layer, but in such small amounts that the upper layer would remain potable most of the way to the Virginia Capes. But the tide is there. The great mass of water in the Bay sloshes back and forth at speeds that reach 2 knots. The flows are turbulent and tear great globs from both layers. From the upper layer globs are carried down into the lower layer, and globs from the lower layer are transferred to the upper. There they mix so that the "fresh" upper layer becomes increasingly salty toward the mouth of the Bay while the "salty" lower layer becomes increasingly fresh toward the head, yet at any given place in the Bay the lower layer is always saltier and denser than the upper layer. The difference in salinity between the two layers is nearly the same over much of the length of the Bay.

The sea salt mixed into the upper layer is discharged, mixed with the fresh river water, back into the sea. If this attrition of the lower layer were to go on without compensation, the river would win a quick victory. The entire Bay would soon be "fresh" from top to bottom. The sea would have been eliminated. But this has not happened. While the total inventory of salt in the system varies seasonally and somewhat from year to year, its average salinity has remained essentially unchanged for thousands of years. There must be a supply of salt, an inexhaustible supply. And there is: the sea. For every part of it that is driven out, it has a replacement. Compared to the Bay, the sea is infinite; its volume is 20 million times greater. A slow, persistent current moves silently up the Bay in the lower layer to resupply the salt that has been flushed out to sea in the upper layer.

We have seen that the rivers must discharge their water to the ocean. On the average, the rivers entering the Bay must get rid of 70,000 cubic feet every second. However, when we measure the discharge to the ocean in the upper layer through the mouth of the Bay, we find the discharge is not 70,000 cubic feet per second, but that it averages about 700,000 cubic feet per second, ten times as much. This excess water is water transported from the lower layer to the upper layer by a steady vertical flow which occurs along the entire length of the estuary. This vertical motion, called the "entrainment velocity," transports water and salt from the lower layer into the upper layer. Random, turbulent motions also occur. On the average, they do not produce a net transport of water, but do lead to a net transport of salt from the higher salinity lower layer to the fresher upper layer. Since the amount of water in the Bay has changed very little from week to week, from year to year, or even from century to century over at least the past several thousand years, it is clear that the flow of sea water into the Bay in the lower layer must be nine times the fresh water flow of all the rivers that enter it. The net difference in the flows of two layers through the Capes must equal the total fresh water input to the Bay; no more, no less, if the volume of the Bay is to be maintained. Since the total fresh water input to the Bay varies seasonally and from year to year, the total net discharge through the mouth of the Bay also changes, but not by a great deal. The ratio of the discharge of the upper layer to the fresh water input also varies seasonally and

from year to year, but roughly inversely to the variation in fresh water input. As a result, the volume rate of outflow of the upper layer does not vary greatly.

We have, then, the oscillatory tidal flow which is the dominant circulation pattern in the Bay. Part of the potential energy of this highly organized, periodic flow is dissipated through the kinetic energy of the highly disorganized, aperiodic, random turbulent motions which mix the fresh water and the sea water. The resulting density field drives a second highly organized flow pattern—the estuarine circulation. It is this slower, more subtle circulation that moves water persistently seaward in the upper layer and landward in the lower layer at speeds of only about one-fifth those of the stronger tidal currents that is in many respects the more important circulation pattern. We observe these kinds of circulation patterns not only in the Bay proper, but in each of its larger tributary estuaries.

Our sketch of the arena is almost complete, except that we have not mentioned that the struggle between river and sea takes place on a carousel; the Earth rotates. As a result, in the northern hemisphere, every motion is deflected to its right. The upper seaward flowing layer is bent toward the western shore of the Bay while the lower landward flowing layer is bent toward the Eastern Shore. The upper layer is thicker to the west and the lower layer thicker to the east. The division between them is thus not level. It slopes upward to the east. As a result, along any horizontal east-west line across the Bay, salinity increases eastward and the water is saltier along the Eastern Shore.

The fluctuating force of the Susquehanna constantly plays against the encroaching sea; the fresh water, driven by gravity, presses against the leading edge of the invading sea water. When the river is in spate, it forces the sea to retreat. When river flow decreases, the sea rebounds, advancing quickly to reclaim its territory. So the skirmish line sways back and forth with the seasons. The Susquehanna runs most strongly in late winter and early spring, when water that has been locked up in snow and ice over much of Pennsylvania and New York is suddenly freed to add to the warm spring rains that feed it. The sea retreats nearly to Tolchester. Summer drought robs the river of munitions and permits the sea, albeit a dilute one, to advance to Turkey Point at the head of the Bay and beyond. In late fall, rains once again bring a lesser renewal of fresh water and the sea again retreats, only to advance once more as winter locks up the water throughout the drainage basin of the Susquehanna. Once in a while the river finds an ally in a tropical storm. In June 1972, Tropical Storm Agnes gave the Susquehanna enough ammunition to drive the sea all the way back to Annapolis, farther seaward than had ever been recorded by man.

The struggle between river and sea has created something that is neither river nor sea. We call this new thing an "estuary," meaning "a semi-enclosed coastal body of water, freely connected to the ocean and within which sea water is mixed with and measurably diluted by fresh water from the land." An estuary is like nothing else. Within this dynamic environment, only a relatively small number of organisms can thrive, but those that do are found in greater abundance, area for area, than anywhere else on Earth. Around it, by choice, cluster people in their millions.

It may seem as though the sea has everything on its side and that the river has nothing to fight with; that the river has no recourse but to wait patiently and passively for the next drop in sea level to reclaim its territory. Not so. In the river's arsenal is one weapon, a weapon better for a war of attrition than for a frontal assault, one which will ultimately win, even if the level of the sea remains where it is, so long as the river continues to run to the sea. That weapon is sediment.

When the last ice age ended, it left behind an extensive cover of unsorted debris—boulders, rocks, gravel, sand, silt, clay—glacial till. The debris left in the wake of the glacier blanketed most of the drainage basin of the Susquehanna, in places to a thickness of more than 1,000 feet, and to an average of several tens of feet. The leading edge of the glacier bit into the land like the blade of a plow unfurling the earth before it, as it advanced. When it began its retreat it left a mound of material that wound its way for hundreds of miles through Pennsylvania and New York; a mound that marked the farthest advance of the glacier. Ice is indiscriminate; water in its liquid form is more selective. But flowing water would have to work for hundreds, even thousands, of years to sort out and file the materials left in this enormous chaotic mass. Streams fed by the melting glacier set about the job. Boulders and cobbles they could roll—the larger ones only during extreme floods. The smaller sand grains could be bounced along. The finer particles of silt and clay could be held in suspension for long periods before settling out; they moved with the water. Thus, the water sorted the debris by size, with the largest rocks nearest the places where they were dropped by the glacier and the smallest silt and clay particles farthest downstream. Floodwaters sometimes carried particles out of the river valley and up onto the bordering flood plains where they were left when the waters withdrew. There the particles would remain, sometimes for centuries, waiting for the next flood to rescue them and send them once again on their way downstream. While the filing system has remained the same throughout geological time, the locations of the appropriate compartments have shifted with the level of the sea.

Before sea level rose and while the rivers still meandered across the exposed continental shelf, most of the finer particles of silt and clay were carried through what is now the Bay across the continental shelf, and were deposited on the continental slope. The coarser sand and gravel came to rest on the continental shelf. The rocks and boulders lagged behind, strewn all the way back to the old glacier's edge.

As sea level rose and the sea moved landward, the sites of deposition moved with it. Fine particles began to accumulate in the stream valleys cut by the James and the Susquehanna prior to the encroachment of the sea. The surf moved like lines of bulldozers, churning the old shelf deposits, destroying the geological record, and spreading a uniform blanket of sand over the shelf.

As the sea invaded the Bay, it swiftly transformed the broad river valley from a region where erosion had been dominant into an estuary where deposition is dominant. Almost none of the sediment carried by the Susquehanna and its tributaries now reaches the sea. It is all trapped within the Bay and deposited there.

Fine particles carried into the Bay by the Susquehanna settle slowly as they move toward the sea. Shuffled back and forth by the tides, they may seem to be going nowhere, but each particle in the upper layer ends each tidal cycle a little farther seaward because of the slow seaward flow of the upper layer. It also finds itself a little deeper in the water because it sinks a little faster than mixing carries it upward. However, once it reaches the lower layer, its movement reverses direction. Nature has played a trick on it, thwarting its trip to the sea. Still carried back and forth by the tidal currents, it now ends each cycle a little closer to the head of the Bay. The sediment is carried back toward its source, the Susquehanna. This mechanism creates a sediment trap in the upper Bay north of Tolchester where the upstream flow of the lower layer peters out. Beneath the trap, a delta is forming; not a classic triangular delta, but a delta none the less. Sedimentation in the trap is more than 10 times faster than it is farther seaward. The Susquehanna is fighting back with the only weapon it has—sediment—to drive back the intruder, to expel the sea from its basin.

The same mechanism is at work in each of the major estuaries tributary to the Bay. In all of them, sedimentation rates are much greater near their heads than farther seaward. Each is pushing the sea toward the Bay proper while the Susquehanna pushes it seaward.

Even with the two-layered estuarine circulation pattern and its sediment trap, one might expect that most of the sediment would be carried through the Bay and out to sea because the particles are so small; because they sink so slowly. Laboratory experiments in still water show that their average settling rate is less than three feet per day. Since there is a vertical entrainment flow associated with the two-layered estuarine circulation pattern, the particles are subject to an upward mixing velocity of nearly the same magnitude as their settling rates. The particles may be falling through the water, but the water itself is moving up just about as fast as single particles should be moving down. In addition, turbulent motions, although producing equal upward and downward velocities, function through a complex process called "non-linear interaction" to retard the settling of particles. Why, then, should they not remain always in the upper layer and ultimately reach the sea? We find that particles sink much more rapidly than can be accounted for by what we know of the settling rates of single particles. In the Bay, particles appear to sink, not as individual particles, but as agglomerates, as groups of particles bound together. The result is a larger "particle," a faster settling rate, and an increase in the sedimentation rate.

But how are these agglomerated particles formed? Turbulent motion causes the fine particles to dance about in a random fashion, first one way, then another, increasing the probability that they will collide. It is much like the Brownian motion of very, very fine particles. Once particles collide, they can be held together by physical and chemical forces. But it is living organisms which play perhaps the most important role in agglomerating particles.

Many of the animals that live in the Bay's waters and on its floor obtain their food by filtering out fine organic particles suspended in the water. For example, copepods, tiny crustaceans less than 0.04 inches long, which are one of the Bay's most abundant forms of zooplankton, are filter feeders. Each copepod filters material from some 3 to 16 ounces of Bay water each day. With average concentrations as great as 10 copepods per quart of Bay water, it is clear that a volume of water equivalent to the entire volume of the Bay is being processed by filtering copepods alone every few days. Filter feeders try to be selective and, indeed, have sophisticated ways of distinguishing edible from inedible particles, organic from inorganic, and large from small. But in the upper Bay, the soup is so thick, the particle concentrations so great, that selection has to take place within the gut. As in eating stew, it is hard to avoid the less appetizing ingredients. The rejected inorganic particles passed through the gut are agglomerated and compacted; transformed into composite particles that sink much more rapidly than their individual components. Copepods are only one of hundreds of kinds of filter feeders at work in the Bay. Filter feeders are a most effective part of the Bay's sediment processing system.

Rivers are not the only source of sediments. Shore erosion, the sea itself, biological activity within the Bay, and municipal and industrial discharges all add their bit. The sources of sediment may thus be external, internal, or marginal to the Bay. The Bay itself is the giant processor. It sorts the material, shifts it from place to place, reworks it by waves, tidal currents, and organisms—sometimes over and over—before depositing it in its "final" resting place.

Man has altered sedimentation in the Bay but only within the last 350 years. Until the early colonists arrived in the 1600s, there was little agriculture; lush vegetation covered the rolling landscape that surrounds the Bay. Leaves broke the force of rain and wind, robbing them of their erosive power. Roots bound the topsoil. But the colonists would change that. They stripped the rich soil of this protective cover, clearing hundreds of thousands of acres with fire and axe. Their principal crop, tobacco, was hard on the land, robbing it of its essential nutrients within a few years. Then it was "move on." The exhausted fields were simply abandoned, left bare to be stripped of topsoil by wind and rain. The sediment loads to the Bay after farm-

ing began increased more than fourfold, from less than 100 tons per square mile per year to 400 or even 850 tons per square mile per year. Once clear streams now ran brown. Captain John Smith's Bay, where you could see bottom in 50 feet of water, became our Bay, where you can seldom see bottom even when you are hard and fast aground.

The soil stripped from the exposed land was carried by streams and rivers into the Bay and particularly into its tributaries. Even before 1800, siltation was a serious problem; sediments choked the shallow harbors. In the early 1700s, Joppa Town at the mouth of the Little Gunpowder River in the upper Bay was the county seat of Baltimore County and Maryland's most important and prosperous seaport. By 1750, shoaling seriously interfered with the operation of the port and its importance waned. In 1763 the county seat was moved to Baltimore. Today the only remainder of that once thriving seaport is hidden by underbrush more than 2 miles from navigable water: stone mooring posts that once secured the hawsers of majestic seagoing ships. Upper Marlboro on the Patuxent and Port Tobacco on the river of the same name fared no better.

But inept colonial farming was not the only culprit. It is estimated that the sediment yield of the Susquehanna drainage basin was 10 to 30 times greater at the peak of coal mining and agricultural activity in the 19th century than it is today. More recently, clearance of land for urbanization and suburbanization sent sediment yields soaring to a hundred times their natural, pre-colonial levels.

The Bay is aging rapidly on a geological time scale; it is being filled in with sediments. The deltas forming in the upper Bay and in the upper reaches of each of its tributaries are growing slowly but persistently seaward. As they grow, they are extending the realms of their rivers, forcing the sea ever so slowly back. Eventually the in-filling of the Bay will be complete and the Susquehanna will have recaptured its tributaries and will wind to the sea across a broad depositional plain. The struggle will have ended in victory for the river.

If the sea remains at its present level, and if all of the sediment discharged to the Bay is trapped within it, the Bay will be filled within 10,000 to 20,000 years and another estuary will have vanished. If sea level rises, the life of the estuary will be prolonged. If sea level falls, its life will be shortened. The death of the estuary is certain, with or without man. Other "bays" died before man even came to the Bay country. The "Bay" has died many deaths, only to be reborn on the next swing of sea level.

The milieu

There is nothing permanent except change.
—Heraclitus

As the sea invaded the ancestral river valley to form an estuary, the kinds of inhabitants changed. Some salt water animals and plants came in with the sea; some fresh water forms retreated to the upper reaches; still others crept into the estuary from its margins to examine, and sometimes to settle in this new and unfamiliar environment. Few remained to take up permanent residence. The estuary is a battlefield between sea and river, and active combat makes life difficult for those who wander into the line of fire.

The Chesapeake Bay and other estuaries are perhaps the most dynamic aquatic environments on earth. Physical and chemical properties change, and change quickly, and they show abrupt changes within short distances, both vertically and horizontally. A striped bass descending vertically through a mere 30 feet may pass through waters that differ in salinity* by 10 parts per thousand (10‰), in temperature by 10°F, in suspended sediment concentration by a thousand-fold, and in dissolved oxygen from saturation to almost none. Few organisms can tolerate such changes.

If our striped bass swims horizontally, the changes it meets are less abrupt but still substantial. A 10‰ change in salinity might be encountered only after several miles, and only then in the upper reaches of the Bay and its tributaries. However, compared with the open ocean where it would have to swim from equator to pole, more than 5,000 nautical miles, to encounter a similar change in salinity, the Bay is still a place of extremes.

Our bass cannot avoid change even by hovering in one place. It will still endure changes that are just as large if it stays in the same place long enough. There is no escape. All the prop-

---

*Salinity can be defined as the mass of dissolved solids in a unit mass of water. It is expressed as the number of grams of solids dissolved in a kilogram of water. This is equivalent to parts per thousand and is represented by the symbol ‰.

erties that surround it, controlling its life in the Bay, can change more within a few hours or a few days than they do in much of the open ocean away from its near-surface layer during weeks, months, years, decades, or even centuries. Near the bottom of the Bay the concentration of sediment suspended within the water changes by as much as a thousand-fold every few hours as tidal currents ebb, go slack, and flood again, alternately eroding and depositing the Bay's soft, fine-grained sediments. In the upper reaches of the Bay and each of its tributaries near the transition from river to estuary, changes in salinity of 8 to 10‰ occur with the rhythm of the tides as they sweep the front separating fresh and brackish water back and forth. Changes with longer periods come with the seasons. Surface temperatures in the Bay rise above 85°F in the summer and fall below 32°F in the winter. Near bottom, temperatures oscillate from 75°F to 35°F.

The only thing constant about the Chesapeake Bay is constant change.

The varieties of life in the ocean seem almost infinite. But most of them die quickly if the environment to which they are adapted changes ever so slightly. Relatively few species can survive the stresses of an environment as changeable as the Bay. The result is that the variety of life forms in the Bay is limited, almost monotonous. It is as if a jungle contained only dogs, cats, and mice; no aardvarks, giraffes, or chimpanzees. Even though the Bay contains within itself conditions that range from nearly full oceanic to fresh water, its range of life does not equal the sum of that of the sea and the rivers that formed it. But what the Bay lacks in variety, it more than makes up for in sheer numbers. Species that can tolerate Bay conditions have often left behind in the ocean their natural predators, who are unable to survive in the estuary. Food is abundant in this giant cornucopia; for those who can thrive in the Bay's harsh environment, it proves to be the promised land.

Not all the kinds of creatures adapted to the Bay live there all the time, although some do.

There are others that enter from the river or from the sea for short periods, to forage or to breed, and some that use the Bay as a nursery for their young. But even those species that pass their entire lives within the Bay are not truly "estuarine." How could they be? Estuaries appear and disappear. Their residents have been evicted many times during the eons and still the species have persisted. They can live in open coastal waters, even if not so opulently. "Estuarine" forms are, in fact, marine forms that happen to be able to tolerate low salinities and wide fluctuations in environmental properties. They are not highly specialized in form and function. They are generalists, capable of seizing an opportunity and exploiting it. Few in kind, they are present in enormous numbers, making the Bay one of the most productive areas on earth.

If a community of living things is to sustain itself and thrive, it must have a balance among three functions: production, consumption, and decomposition. The producers assemble inorganic nutrient material from the air, the water, and the sediments and, using the energy of the sun, photosynthesize it into more complex living organic matter. Without some check, producers would multiply without bound to choke the entire living space and no cycle could be established. Consumers keep producers in check by eating them and, incidentally, reorganizing their living matter into even more complex forms. But again, no cycle will be started. When the inorganic matter is used up, the system grinds to a halt and dies. To complete the cycle, we need the decomposers, the recyclers, which break down dead organic matter into forms that can be used again by the producers. If production, consumption, and decomposition are in a proper balance, the cycle rolls on and on. Systems like the Bay, having few working parts and few pathways, are vulnerable to interference with any of their parts. Break one link and the cycle may falter. The cycle in the Bay, being a natural one, adjusts well to changing natural conditions. It is much less able to survive man-made changes, which tend to be more bizarre and persistent. But for now the system hums.

The Bay is one of the most productive bodies of water in the world; far more so than the rivers that flow into it or the sea into which it empties. Its circulation, which traps sediments within it, the sediments that will destroy it in the end, also concentrates the nutrients that stimulate plant growth. These plants, the primary producers, so called because only they can transmute inorganic carbon dioxide and nutrients into living tissue—organic carbon—are, therefore, the ultimate source of food for all the consumers in the cycle. They are the base of the food web. They are the submerged rooted aquatic plants that grow in the shallows; the marsh grasses that grow along the margins, alternately exposed and submerged; and most important of all, the microscopic plants, the phytoplankton, that float in their myriads within the water column. Small they may be, but in their astronomical numbers, a huge mass of food, a floating factory of impressive proportions. It is on such plants that all other life in the Bay ultimately depends for food.

The activity of this photosynthetic food factory is called primary productivity, a rate of production given as the average amount of carbon fixed per unit of surface area during one year. Photosynthesis can take place within the water column only to the depth to which sunlight penetrates, that is, within the euphotic zone. In the upper Bay, during periods of high runoff from the Susquehanna when its waters are charged with fine particles stripped from the soil, the thickness of the euphotic zone may be considerably less than one foot. In the middle and lower Bay, it is usually 30 feet or more. Neither of these is particularly impressive when compared with an open-ocean thickness of 300 feet or more. One might suppose that the ocean should be more productive than the Bay, because for each unit of surface area, it has at least 10 times more depth, 10 times more room, where drifting microscopic plants can grow. Not so. The Bay's primary productivity is ten to one hundred times that of the open ocean.

With primary production high, the larder is full, and secondary production, that of the consumers, does equally well. Little of the Bay's green "grass" goes to waste. It is grazed off, packaged into larger, more complex units and passed up the food chain to more highly organized consumers. There are herbivores, the grazers on the floating meadows of plankton and on the strands of grass, that eat nothing but green things. There are the carnivores that prey on other animals. And there are the omnivores that will eat anything that comes their way. These consumers range in size from the microscopic zooplankton, drifting in the water, up through the nekton—the fishes that cruise the Bay in search of prey—and on to human beings who tend to think of the ecology of the Bay in terms of what they themselves like to catch and eat. "Save our Stripers." "Eat Clams and Live Longer." "Eat Oysters and Love Longer." But success of the consumers depends, ultimately, upon the success of those plants that can be seen only with a microscope.

The secondary production of the Bay is prodigious. For comparison, Georges Bank off Cape Cod, one of the world's best fishing grounds, yields less than three tons of fish per square mile per year. The Bay yields nearly twelve. But that is not all; some of the fish harvested on Georges Bank owe their existence to the Bay.

Large numbers of anadromous fishes—those going upstream from the sea at breeding time—spawn their eggs in the Bay, and the juveniles return to the sea to restock the fisheries of the Atlantic continental shelf. Others, spawned in the ocean, enter the Bay for a time only to rejoin the offshore schools in later life. Croaker spawn in continental shelf waters off the mouth of the Bay. The Bay, like a giant vacuum cleaner, sucks the croaker larvae into its lower layer and transports them as far north as Annapolis. There they feed and grow, returning to the sea as juveniles.

It has been estimated that 70 percent of the fishes now found in open Atlantic coastal waters depend on the Chesapeake Bay and on the other estuaries along the Atlantic coast during a part of their life cycles. This sounds impressive, and indeed it is. But what will happen when sea level falls and the estuaries fill in? The answer seems to be that in the past, when there were no estuaries, the species survived in the open sea, but in far fewer numbers than today; so few, in fact, that it is inconceivable that they could have sustained a commercial fishery. Any serious loss of area from the Bay, or any serious degradation of its habitability, whether arising from natural causes or from human intervention, will have wide-ranging repercussions on our fisheries, repercussions by no means limited to the fisheries carried out within the margins of the Bay.

More nutrients, more primary producers; more primary production, more secondary production. Enough recyclers, even more nutrients. And the cycle spins merrily on; faster and faster. There must be some speed limit.

The numbers and kinds of plants in the Bay are controlled, principally, by the abundance of the several kinds of nutrients and, to a lesser extent, by the forms in which they are present. Fertilizer is good, more fertilizer is better. But only up to a point. Once the "broth" becomes too rich, the composition of species alters. The balance is delicate, and changes can be rapid. Desirable plants vanish to be replaced by less desirable plants, the "weeds" of the Bay. Since these are not eaten, they accumulate. In low-salinity reaches of the Bay, the shift is usually to the blue-green algae. In more saline areas, diatoms may be replaced by less desirable dinoflagellates and green algae. More is no longer better. Enrichment has become eutrophication. There are intense blooms alternating with mas-

sive die-offs which send dissolved oxygen crashing to near-zero levels. That makes it hard for anything to breathe, and more death follows.

The changes begin with the microscopic floating plants, the phytoplankton, but they don't stop there. Subtle shifts in the assemblages of phytoplankton to smaller forms can be reflected in changes running all the way through the food web up to the finfish and shellfish we harvest. Fortunately, estuarine phytoplankton communities are less susceptible to alteration by increased nutrient levels than are those found in fresh water. The mixture of salt and fresh water buffers the system against change. Most of the Bay's plants are desirable; there are relatively few weed patches. But weeds are there and in just the places one would expect them to be; in the upper reaches of the Bay and, particularly, in its tributaries. They are found in areas where waters are fresh or only slightly brackish, in areas where nutrients from rivers are high, and in areas where the natural circulation concentrates nutrients, sediments, and particle-associated contaminants.

The patterns of degradation resulting from human activities and from the natural sedimentary aging process are similar. Both move from the upper reaches of the Bay and its tributaries toward the ocean while encroaching from its margins. Although the patterns are similar, the rates at which they advance are different. At present, degradation from human sources is outrunning sedimentation, and we have reason for concern that we will lose the Bay long before it disappears.

The marshes

Ye marshes, how candid and simple and nothing
  withholding and free,
Ye publish yourselves to the sky and offer
  yourselves to the sea!
  —Sidney Lanier, *The Marshes of Glynn*

As the sea invaded the Bay basin 10,000 years ago, it mixed with the fresh river water. The diluted sea soon spilled out of the narrow, deep, ancestral Susquehanna River channel and flowed out across the sandy valley floor. Each small rise in sea level sent water scurrying across the gentle slopes to inundate existing fresh water marshes, and to lap against forests of spruce and hemlock. Most animals can move, and those beat a hasty retreat from the briny invader. The plants and those animals that could not, died quickly.

The sea toyed with the land. Sea level—rising or falling—is seldom at "sea level." The sea surface oscillates eternally about its average position; in the Bay, with a period of slightly more than half a day. This daily tidal rise and fall of the sea surface is much larger and more rapid than the long-term change in sea level. The first is a response to the wanderings of the moon and the sun; the second to the advances and retreats of the great continental ice sheets. The tide may change the level of the sea surface by more than a foot in an hour; glacial movements may take a century, or more, to effect a comparable change. The tide changes the direction in which the sea surface moves every six hours. Rise in world-wide sea level changes to fall with the rhythm of the ponderous succession of the ice ages—tens of thousands of years. Both the quick and the slow changes in the level of the sea surface are important to the formation and maintenance of the Bay's marshes. The slowly changing average position of the sea surface, sea level, determines where our marshes will be; the swiftly changing tidal fluctuations about sea level determine their extent.

The sea claimed new territory with each increment it rose. With every flood tide the sea sent salty fingers darting across extensive shoals deep into creeks, only to retract them on the succeeding ebb tide. As the sea continued to rise, its penetration into the terrestrial domain increased in space and in time. The period of each drowning was prolonged, the penetration deeper. Elevations of the valley floor became islands just before they became shoals. High sections of peninsulas were cut off from the mainland, transformed into islands that floated in the growing estuary.

The Eastern Shore offered little resistance. Its low-lying coastal areas, the gentle slopes of its streams and rivers, and their small discharges were no match for the swelling sea. In the contest between sea and land, the sea was winning. Sea level was rising all the time. It still is, although its pace has slackened to only an inch or so in a decade—less than one-quarter of what it was between 15,000 and 5,000 years ago.

Submerged areas of the valley floor that did not build up at the same rate as that at which the sea rose were permanently drowned. Few areas could keep pace for long. Those that could were always along the margins, along the leading edge of the sea, and in the fringes around islands, in protected areas where waters were shoal, where tidal currents and wave energy were reduced. It was in these areas where plants could take root and unite with the land in its battle against the sea. The armies of green were few, but their numbers large.

Only a few land plants could survive the salty sea, albeit a dilute one. Few could tolerate having their roots almost constantly bathed in salt water and their leaves submerged twice each day, and then left high and dry to be baked in the hot summer sun or chilled by the cold winter wind. Of the thousands of species of plants that inhabit the land only three species of grass, *Spartina alterniflora, Spartina patens,* and *Distichlis spicata* could thrive. Then, as now, the *Spartinas* dominated all east coast salt marshes, by mass and by areal coverage.

Spartina alterniflora, commonly called cordgrass, is the more common of the two species. It is a large, coarse grass with leaves up to one inch wide at the base and extending to five feet, or more, in height. It grows best where tidal currents are relatively strong. Because cordgrass can tolerate submergence for much longer periods than *Spartina patens* and other marsh plants, it could survive longer than other marsh plants

after the sea had passed over it. It could retain a foothold as long as the sea was drained away for at least a few hours each tidal cycle. Because of its greater tolerance to submergence in salt water, cordgrass enabled marshes to develop over at least the upper two-thirds of the intertidal zone. And it could pioneer expansion of saltmarsh into other, virgin, areas. Seeds blown onto mud flats exposed at low tide could germinate and take root. Clumps of *Spartina alterniflora* marsh torn away by storm waves or ice could serve as nuclei for development of new marsh. But even cordgrass could not survive continuous submergence of its roots in standing water. This sensitivity limited its seaward extension into the Bay, and precluded growth in those areas of the marsh where standing water was retained in puddles and ponds because of topographic features. Barren, unvegetated puddle areas in the interior of a marsh are called *pannes.*

Spartina patens is a fine, small grass rarely exceeding a quarter of an inch across and two feet in height. It grows best high on the marsh. Colonists called it salt meadow hay and harvested it to feed their livestock.

Sea lavender and other exotic marsh plants bloomed among the *Spartinas.* While adding little to the total mass of plants and to their coverage, they contributed disproportionately to the beauty and variety of the marsh.

Once established, the marsh plants' roots and rhizomes bound the soil, increasing its resistance to erosion. The plant-stems baffled the energy of the waves and the tides, quieting the waters. No longer capable of carrying the loads of suspended matter they bore, the waters released a heavy rain of fine particles of mud and organic matter onto the surface of the marsh. Dead and decaying marsh grasses were added locally and incorporated into the marsh, along with roots, rhizomes, and stems. The level of the marsh slowly built up, like the cities of today that hoist themselves on their own garbage and trash. If the rate of marsh build-up kept pace with the rising sea, the marsh survived. If it did not, the marsh was drowned; eventually covered with mud and buried beneath the Bay floor.

The rate of accretion of marshes is tuned to the rate of rise of sea level. The more rapid the rise, the longer the marsh is submerged on each flood tide. The more prolonged each submergence, the greater the opportunity to trap sedimentary particles and organic matter to add to its surface. The longer the submergence, the greater the trapping of sediment, the more rapid the sedimentation rate, the greater the rate of build-up. But the feedback mechanism favors the maintenance of the marsh only to a point. When the rate of rise of sea level exceeds some threshold, the marsh is sent to a watery grave.

None of the marshes formed during the initial stages of development of the modern Chesapeake Bay estuary survived. The rise of sea level was too rapid; the sediment inputs too small. Remains of previous marshes are contained within the layers of sediment that make up the Bay's bottom—the graveyard of its past. Ancient marsh deposits appear as layers of organic-rich sediments, as peat, charged with gas bubbles produced by the degradation of organic matter and entrapped within the sediments. Gone but not forgotten.

As the Bay evolved with continued rise of the sea, new marshland formed landward of that which had been drowned. New marshes were extended inland over the edges of what had been fastland. Older marshes were drowned and left in the wake of the advancing sea of green grass. Fresh water grasses, shrubs and trees were engulfed by the diluted sea water, eliminated, and replaced by marsh grasses.

The Bay's marshes of today developed within the past 3,000 to 5,000 years; only after the rate of rise of sea level slowed appreciably. Wherever the rising sea touched, there was the potential for marsh development. The sea was the driving force—the stimulus—the marsh only one of several possible responses, a response that was not realized everywhere the sea extended its reach. Other necessary conditions were not always met. In many areas the water was too deep; the sedimentary bed too mobile; or the area too exposed to waves and tidal currents for plants to gain and maintain a foothold.

In favorable areas, marshes did form. Lamina by lamina, layer by layer, they accreted; a little on each tidal cycle. Two tidal cycles a day for five thousand years—3,650,000 tidal cycles in all; 3,650,000 flood tides. Over that span of 5,000 years, over those 3,650,000 flood tides, sea level rose approximately 15 feet. To keep pace, a marsh had to accrete an average of only three hundred thousandths of an inch on each flood tide, a layer less than one fine-grained mud particle in thickness. An infinitesimal amount, but an amount that could not be sustained in many of the Bay's fringing areas, at least not until the colonists arrived.

Colonists stripped hundreds of thousands of acres of virgin forest. Grasses and trees were replaced by tobacco and corn, leaving bare earth, devoid of any plant cover, exposed for months at a stretch. And when the fields were depleted of nutrients, they were abandoned; left bare to be robbed of soil by wind and rain. Sediment inputs to the Bay and particularly to its tributaries shot up five, ten, even one hundred times. Downstream, once clear waters ran muddy. Submerged aquatic vegetation, not marsh plants, but plants like eelgrass that grow permanently submerged, no longer reached by the sun, were killed by the advancing darkness. Extensive beds of submerged plants, plants that added precious oxygen to the waters, were eliminated from the Potomac and elsewhere. Oxygen levels fell. Natural channels shoaled.

Mudflats sprang up along the margins of the Bay where sandy shores had been only a few years before. Many of them were transformed into wetlands—marshes—by colonization of marsh grasses. The marshes were the principal beneficiaries of man's assault on the land. They had found a new ally in their struggle against the rising sea. Plants captured the moving sediment, halting its transfer out into the deeper parts of the Bay, bringing it to rest near shore.

As nearshore environments built up, new habitats were created that provided shelter and food for many of the Bay's animals. New places for the blue crab to hide each time it shed its protective shell. New places for the silverside to breed. New areas for the young striped bass and menhaden to feed in peace, hidden away from predators. New grazing areas for rafts of ducks and gaggles of geese that came from thousands of miles away each winter—many to stay out the winter, others to rest and refuel before continuing their journey to marshes farther south. The Bay's marshes are a link in an important chain that extends for thousands of miles. But, not all saw the benefits in these new environments in colonial days.

Many, perhaps most, failed to recognize the redeeming ecological qualities of the new habitats. They were a nuisance; places where mosquitoes, greenheads, and deerflies bred. They could neither be cultivated, nor built upon. Extensive mudflats and marshes denied people easy access to their docks and to their shores. They were unsightly and they stank. They were neither land nor water. They were what their name implied—wetlands. The band of green that bordered the Bay extended and widened until it seemed to be taking over the Bay. No longer would Father White have written of the Potomac, as he had in 1630—only 150 years before—"This is the sweetest and greatest river I have seene. . . . There are noe marshes or swamps about it, but solid firme ground."

If the Bay's encroaching wetlands were seen then to have little, if any, redeeming value, and be rather a nuisance, something to be gotten rid of, that, too, would change. Soon what had been created to a large degree by people's negligence in their role as custodians of the land and what had been the object of their scorn would be treasured and protected by those who claimed custody of the Bay.

Area for area, wetlands are the Bay's most productive environments. Giant green factories, teeming with green things, large and small. Plants grow everywhere: underwater, above water, in and out of water, even on top of each other. Little growing space is wasted. Submerged grasses, the seagrasses, grow off the edge of the marsh below the water line where they are submerged at all stages of the tide. Seagrasses aren't really "grasses" at all.

Just slightly landward of these in the intertidal zone begin the real grasses. They grow in the zone alternately drowned and drained by salt water; first wet, then dry, twice a day. These are the emergent grasses, the marsh grasses, *Spartina alterniflora* and *Spartina patens*. They extend well up onto the marsh, to its landward limit where they are drowned only on spring tides, the largest tides, which occur when sun and season conspire at new moon and full moon.

Tiny single-celled plants grow on the surface of the mud, particularly on the banks and bottoms of the tidal creeks that cut through the marsh. Invisible to the naked eye as individual plants, they impart a green or golden brown hue to the mud, making it glisten. These are the benthic microalgae.

Other plants grow suspended in the waters that bathe the marsh, moving in and out with the tides. These plants don't really belong to the marsh. They come and go. Their only allegiance is to the water that carries them. These are the phytoplankton.

Then there are the small plants that grow piggy-back on the larger plants. Single-celled algae that attach themselves to the stalks of grasses, hanging on for dear life as the grasses are whipped alternately by currents of wind and water. These are the epiphytic algae.

The contributions of all these kinds of plants add up to a primary productivity among the highest of any of Earth's environments, aquatic or terrestrial. A productivity one hundred times greater than that of the open sea; five times greater than that of the adjacent Bay; three times greater than that of the most productive terrestrial grasslands. The rates of primary production in marshes are at least equivalent to those of the world's most productive grain fields; fields that are carefully tended and nurtured with the best diet technology can provide and money can buy. However, the marsh is not so meticulously attended to, its menu not so carefully planned. The tide and the wind are its cultivators. Sewage and nutrients, washed into the Bay by rivers and streams that drain agricultural areas and septic fields, are its fertilizer. The delivery system is the tide. Twice a day it carries in from the Bay whatever comes along: nutrients and vitamins, sometimes with more than the recommended daily dose of supplements including metals, oils and greases, pesticides, and herbicides. Mealtime is predictable; the menu is potluck. Still, the Bay's marshes generally do well. There is more than enough green grass to go all around.

Some of the marsh's plant life is grazed off directly. Menhaden and pinfish eat eelgrass and marsh grass; birds feed on marsh grass; waterfowl graze on submerged rooted aquatic vegetation; grasshoppers and other insects gnaw on the *Spartinas*; clams and oysters strain out phytoplankton and other organic matter from the rich soup that engulfs them; snails browse along the grass blades, stripping small, single-celled algae that grow on their surfaces. But most of the marsh grasses must die before they can be eaten. Grasses are mostly cellulose, a substance few animals can digest. Once dead, grass is no longer able to protect itself against bacteria and fungi, which immediately attack it, decompose it, break it down into smaller bits and pieces, which animals can eat, and into bacterial and fungal protoplasm, which is easily digested. It is only as detritus, as dead and decaying material, that most organic matter enters the food chain of the marsh. It is a detrital food chain, unlike the grazing food chain of the Bay and the ocean. In some respects, the marsh is similar to the temperate forest where trees and leaves must die and decompose before being eaten. Only after the marsh grass is broken down by bacteria and fungi is it eaten by detritivores; by crabs, worms, snails, small fishes, and other animals with catholic tastes—the marsh's sanitation crew. The marsh is a vegetarian scavenger's paradise, a vegetable boneyard, and it has not gone unnoticed. Not only is primary production—the production of plant tissue—high, secondary production—the production of animal tissue—is high also. Animals are there in large numbers albeit in limited variety. The chow is good if you can stand the hassle.

Conditions on the marsh are even more variable than are those in the adjacent Bay. Not only do the properties of the waters that bathe the marsh change, but the waters are withdrawn completely twice each day as well. First drowned, then drained. First water, then land. Bathed in summer by the cool waters of the Bay each high tide, then baked by the sun on the succeeding low tide. Temperature at the surface of the marsh may swing through more than 50°F with only six hours separating the extremes. Torn by storm waves, swept by cold winds, pelted by rain and hail, gouged by ice. And then there are people. Hunters and fishermen who trample the marsh in search of their prey. Wetland watchers who come to photograph, or just to walk and enjoy.

Few organisms can tolerate the range and frequency of insults. The rigors of permanent residence on the marsh are too much. As in the estuary, the variety of life is monotonous, particularly on the marsh proper. Probably only a half dozen or so species of animals spend their entire life cycles here, and only twice that number pass their adult lives here. Among these are the fiddler crabs, square-backed crabs, and snails. The variety of life on the mudflats is somewhat greater than that on the marsh proper, but still limited. The mudflat is the realm of razor clams, soft and hard clams, bloodworms, clam worms, and lugworms. Few are active both in and out of the water. Most restrict their activity to one mode of life or the other.

Since most animals can choose where they live, most chose to be commuters; to come in from the margins of the marsh to breed, to eat, to hide, but not to stay for long. They enter from the Bay and from the land. Most commuters maintain schedules keyed to the tides.

Those that come by land advance when the tide retreats and retreat when the tide advances. Those that come by sea, advance and retreat in consort with the tide; advancing when it advances, retreating when it retreats. Fish and crabs enter with the sea; insects and shorebirds with its retreat.

Those organisms that take up permanent residence on the marsh and its bordering mud flats must develop either internal mechanisms or modes of behavior to maintain a stable internal environment in the face of a drastically changeable external one. Most animals have the choice; plants do not. Both solutions require the expenditure of large amounts of energy. Many residents burrow into the soft muds of the tidal flats to escape the extremes of the world above, emerging only at certain stages of the tide. Their vertical migrations driven by internal clocks synchronized with the natural driving forces of the sun and the moon, bring them out of their burrows only at low or high tide. A vertical migration of only a fraction of an inch into the mud may reduce the environmental variability manyfold. Surprisingly the movements are not limited to animals. Some benthic algae, diatoms, also migrate vertically, although their trips are more limited than those of the animals. These plants are clearly "vegetable," but behave like "animal," and live in little glass houses made of silica that are "mineral." What a confusing world is the salt marsh.

The Bay's marshes perhaps reached their peak in abundance and diversity during the mid to late 1800s. Since then, fewer new ones have been added, fewer old ones have grown, and many well-established ones have been eliminated. The input of sediment has decreased. Better soil conservation is practiced. Less land is cultivated. Coal mining has waned. Reservoirs constructed along a number of the Bay's rivers trap sediment that would normally reach the Bay. The marshes' supply of ammunition has been rationed just as the sea has once more renewed its assault. Within the past two centuries, the rate of rise of local sea level has increased again, perhaps because the Bay region is subsiding. More conscientious care of the land will require more careful management of the marshes.

It is clear that marshes nurture the Bay's important finfish and shellfish populations, that they provide important habitats for waterfowl, and that they cleanse the Bay, sopping up contaminants from the water, transferring them to the sediments. While now widely recognized, the exact quantitative importance of marshes has not been established; perhaps it can never be done with certainty. Our awareness of their ecological significance came slow and late. Legislation to protect these precious areas was adopted only on July 1, 1970, in Maryland and on July 1, 1972, in Virginia. By then hundreds of thousands of acres of marshland had been destroyed, more than 200,000 acres since the turn of the century alone. Still, many marshes remain; large expansive marshes like Blackwater and Eastern Neck National Wildlife Refuges and countless small ones, approximately 475,000 acres in all. The new legislation has been remarkably effective in limiting the areas of marshland altered each year. In 1979, the State of Maryland received applications for permits to alter only 3.8 acres of State wetlands and 11.5 acres of private wetlands. Permits were granted for only 1.1 and 2.5 acres, respectively.

Salt marshes are among the Bay's most scenic assets, adding a gentleness to the Bay's eastern shore that contrasts sharply with the rugged bluffs of the western shore and with those of the upper Bay. Haunting, eerie, peaceful, lonely. Constantly changing in form and mood, in pattern and outline, in flora and fauna, in sound and smell. The marshes lie along the shoreline like jade beads on a precious necklace.

Four estuarine animals that use the Bay in very different ways

*And I would I could know what swimmeth below
when the tide comes in. . .*
—Sidney Lanier, *The Marshes of Glynn*

Consider four very different animals—the water flea *(Podon polyphemoides)*, the striped bass or rockfish *(Morone saxatilis)*, the American oyster *(Crassostrea virginica)*, and the blue crab *(Callinectes sapidus)*. The last three are well known to everyone having even a casual acquaintance with the Bay. The first is known, probably, only to the scientists who study the Bay, and not even to all of them. The life cycles of all four are intimately tied to the natural biological, chemical, geological, and physical processes that characterize the Bay and by people's impact on them. All four begin life among the plankton—those creatures, both animals and plants, that float and drift with the flow of the waters. Of the four only one, *Podon*, remains planktonic throughout its life. The other three leave the plankton after a few weeks to pursue very different life styles. The striped bass joins the nekton—the fishes—and swims freely throughout much of the Bay and even beyond. The oyster attaches itself to the bottom of the Bay and never again moves unless it happens to be scraped off the bottom by a waterman's tongs or a skipjack's dredge. The blue crab adopts a life style that ties it closely to the bottom, but it retains free movement and uses much of the Bay during its life. The success of each is determined, in large part, by its success while a member of the Bay's plankton.

THE STRIPED BASS OR ROCKFISH
(Morone saxatilis)

Early each spring, in March or April, as water temperatures begin to rise, adult striped bass, ripe with eggs and sperm, move out of the deeper parts of the Bay where they have overwintered in the warmer, deeper waters and make their way back to their spawning grounds in the tidal fresh and slightly brackish waters at the head of the Bay and its tributaries. The spawning instinct of the striped bass is powerful and the drive to reach fresh water strong, but the journey has its hazards. The pathways to the spawning grounds traverse areas that are intensively fished commercially, and many who start will not arrive. The routes are lined with nets strung on poles driven into the Bay's soft bottom. Where shipping lanes preclude fixed nets, free-floating nets drift silently beneath the surface, ready to capture the unwary fish compelled toward their spawning grounds. This catch is prized by fisherman and gourmet alike. The striped bass is Maryland's most valuable and important finfish. Adult female striped bass may reach a length of six feet and weigh as much as 175 pounds. In comparison, the males are puny. Males rarely reach four feet and seldom exceed 100 pounds.

Before the dam at Conowingo was built in 1929, the Susquehanna was the spawning area most favored by striped bass in the whole Chesapeake Bay system. Spawning occurred in the Susquehanna as far upstream as Northumberland and, at times, even beyond. When the pathway to this spawning ground was blocked, the striped bass was forced downstream and retreated to the east. Man eliminated one spawning ground with the Conowingo dam, but he had already created another: the Chesapeake and Delaware Canal. The first C&D Canal, completed in 1829, was a privately owned, locked canal and was of little use to the Bay's fishes. That was to change. In 1919 the federal government bought the canal, enlarged it, and converted it to a sealevel canal. The rebuilt canal was opened on February 25, 1927, and for the first time, during recent geological times at least, there was a free exchange of water between the Chesapeake and Delaware bays and an unimpeded passageway for organisms. Subsequent enlargements increased the intensity of the tidal currents in the Canal and the exchange of water between the two bays.

All favored spawning areas have swift currents where turbulence keeps the eggs afloat, free of sediment, and bathed in waters rich with oxygen. During the spawning season the waters in the Canal are fresh or, at most, only slightly brackish, currents are strong, and flows turbulent. These are ideal conditions for spawn-

ing; conditions that the stripers could hardly have failed to notice. Today the C&D Canal is one of the Bay's most important striped bass spawning areas. Other favored grounds include the upper Bay above Pooles Island, the Susquehanna flats, the upper reaches of the Potomac, the Nanticoke, the Chester, the Choptank, the York, the Rappahannock, and the James.

The males arrive first on the spawning grounds followed closely by the females. Spawning reaches a peak between mid-April and mid-May, triggered by the rapidly rising water temperatures. The waters become alive with thrashing fish. A single mature female casts near the water surface up to several million eggs in a single spawn. Each egg is a nearly perfect, translucent sphere 0.05 to 0.15 inches in diameter, having a density close to that of the surrounding waters. Each female spawns no more than once during a year, completing her task within a few hours and there may be years in which she produces no eggs at all.

Within three to five days of spawning the eggs hatch, and billions of larvae, each 0.1 to 0.2 inches long, wriggle out of their protective egg cases and into the waters of the Bay. These are yolk-sac larvae; each has its own built-in food supply sufficient to nourish it until its jaws develop. Most lie resting on the bottom for the first day or two, recovering from the trauma of hatching. One to three days after hatching many move up to the water surface. Some attach themselves to the undersides of floating objects to conserve their strength for what lies ahead. Their chances of survival are small; less than one in a million. Within a week of hatching their internal food supply is exhausted. If they are to survive, they must forage for themselves, living off the other plankton. Their prey must be large enough to be seen and small enough to swallow. Fortunately for the young striped bass, the Bay is teeming with plankton of suitable size. Many of the larvae forage at the bottom. As they grow larger, stronger, and able to swim against currents, they join the adults in their slow migration down the Bay into low-salinity waters to feed in the shoal areas along the margins of the Bay and its tributaries throughout the summer and fall.

In the late fall, rapid cooling of the surface waters alerts the stripers to the onset of winter. It's time to find a winter habitat. They move away from the shoals and slide silently down into the deeper areas of the Bay where waters will soon be warmer than the near-surface waters they have left behind. They become sluggish but they continue to feed and move about to some extent throughout the winter. They remain in the deeper waters below 50 feet until early spring when, once again, nature calls them back to their spawning grounds. Each will return to the spawning ground where it hatched; the homing instinct is both strong and specific. Year by year the pattern repeats.

About 90 percent of the Bay's striped bass remain within the boundaries of the Chesapeake Bay system during their entire lives. The remaining 10 percent, principally some of the larger fish 2 years old and older, range farther afield. In April and May they leave the Bay, most through the C&D Canal, move down Delaware Bay to the ocean, and migrate northward along the Atlantic coast. Some of them range as far north as Nova Scotia. Even of these, most will retrace their paths through the C&D Canal to return to the Bay between September and December of the same year. A few will remain behind to overwinter along the New England coast.

The striped bass is only one of many semi-anadromous and anadromous fishes that use the Bay's fresh water and brackish water areas for spawning. Others include the American and Hickory shads, the alewife, and several of the herrings. Truly anadromous fishes return to the ocean each year after spawning; the semi-anadromous fishes, like the striped bass, move to more saline waters but, for the most part, remain within the confines of the estuary. Seasonal changes in the Bay trigger their life cycles. They flourish because of the Bay's circulation and productivity—as long as the Bay is not degraded too much by the effluents of society.

THE AMERICAN OYSTER
(Crassostrea virginica)

The American oyster (Crassostrea virginica) is a mollusc that first appeared during the Triassic, 200 million years ago, and which has changed little since. Enormously successful, always unattractive, this creature led Jonathan Swift to remark: "He was a bold man that first ate an oyster." And so he was. But he has had no shortage of imitators. The oyster has been considered a delicacy for millennia. As early as 3,000 years ago, the Chinese savored its succulent meat, and shell middens in the Bay region show that Indians harvested oysters long before white men came. When the British colonists arrived in the early 1600s, they were delighted to find one old friend that reminded them of the finer things they had exchanged for this howling wilderness, and they were quick to exploit it.

The American oyster, a bivalve, is found throughout much of the Bay but principally in water depths of ten to thirty feet. Like the striped bass, the oyster begins life in the plankton. But there the similarity ends.

The sex life of the oyster is nearly as confused as that described in Robert Benchley's famous lecture, "The Sex Life of the Polyp," and accounts, in part, for our abstention from oysters during months without R's. During months without R's, the adult oyster has little interest in sex and, in fact, even less to work with. During the cold weather, its body weight is made up of the glycogen and salts that make it fat and tasty. But in the late spring, the oyster's fancy lightly turns to reproduction and it assumes a sex for the season, or at least part of it. It may be either, primarily. Having made a choice, it converts 80 percent of its body weight to sex organs, which are thin and watery and taste like nothing at all. It isn't that oysters are inedible during the summer; just that they aren't as meaty and succulent. Then too, it's just as well to leave them alone to get on with the business of making more oysters while they are in the mood. In the fall they lose interest and reconvert to glycogen and salts, leaving their sex up for grabs again.

Sexually mature adult oysters release eggs and sperm into the waters of the Bay by the trillions throughout the summer. A single oyster may produce up to 100,000 eggs on a single spawn and may spawn four or five times a summer; a prodigious feat in itself. But it doesn't end there. This same oyster the following season may turn male and emit millions of sperms.

Relatively few eggs are actually fertilized and probably fewer than 1 in 10,000 of those fertilized will survive the larval stage. Within a few days of fertilization the eggs develop into larvae. Each larva has a bivalve shell and cilia (whip-like appendages), which give it some mobility. It is too weak to swim against the Bay's tidal currents and is carried to and fro by the oscillatory motion of the tide. Which way it moves, on the whole, depends upon its depth in the water column. Larvae that spend most of their time in the upper layer are carried seaward. The Bay's circulation concentrates the larvae in the zones of convergence, the regions where moving masses of water come together. The areas of high oyster set are thus controlled by the circulation, that is, by the physics of the system. Historically, among the Bay's best setting areas are the upper reaches of the Manokin, the Piankatank, the James, and the St. Mary's estuaries.

Near the end of the second week, each larva has grown so large, its shell so heavy, that it becomes increasingly difficult for it to keep afloat and propel its mass through the water by beating its hair-like cilia. How would you like to move a waterlogged raft by flailing the water with pieces of rope? The larvae know it's time to find a place to settle down and begin a new, sedentary life; one in keeping with their growing houses. Their mobile homes will not be mobile much longer. The larvae drop to the bottom of the Bay in search of a firm place to set, a place that will support them throughout a lifetime that may last 10 or 20 years, a place that will keep them from sinking into the Bay's soft, muddy sediments to smother in its anoxia as they grow larger and heavier.

Finding a suitable spot to set is the second most critical task of an oyster's life. The first is to avoid being eaten during the planktonic stage. This is one of the few times an oyster must make a decision, and its judgment will affect it for the rest of its life. Fortunately, the larva's sensory powers and vigor are at a peak. They must be. The search is a tough one and the outcome dubious in the extreme. To be between a rock and a hard place would be heaven to an oyster. But finding a rock in Chesapeake Bay is surely as difficult as finding the proverbial needle in a haystack; rocks are virtually non-existent. Even hard places are at a premium.

When the sinking larval oyster reaches bottom, it extends its foot to test the surface—a foot developed especially for that purpose. If the bottom is soft and squishy, he struggles back up into the water, lets the tidal currents drift him for a while, and drops down again hoping for a rock, a bottle, an old tire, an anchor, something, anything firm to set on. More often than not the only hard spot to be had is another oyster, alive or dead. Once satisfied, the larval oyster secretes a small dab of glue from its foot, turns on its side, presses its left shell valve into the glue, and waits. Within 15 minutes the glue has set, and so too has the oyster—for life. Its foot, having served its purpose, is soon absorbed and the oyster begins a new and quite different life. No longer a member of the plankton, it has now joined the benthos, the group of organisms that live on or in the bottom of bodies of water. Once attached, the oyster is literally stuck for life never to move again unless a waterman scrapes him off the bottom.

The newly settled oysters are called spat. Within a month, each will have grown to the size of a pea; within three months, to three inches; within a year, or at most two, he will be sexually mature. From now on we should properly refer to "him" as both he and she—to coin a word "heshe"—but never as "it." Here heshe is. Most oysters start life as males but all spend a large part of their lives alternating between being male and female. A small percentage are functionally hermaphroditic. Who would have thought that the allegedly phlegmatic oyster could be trapped in such hectic sexual confusion?

From now on, heshe must take what the Bay brings. There is little else that heshe can do. If what comes along becomes absolutely intolerable, the only alternative is to close up tightly and wait for things to improve. Soon better water and better food usually come along; but not always soon enough. Oysters that make their homes too close to the mouth of the Susquehanna are intermittently destroyed by unusually high discharges of floodwaters, which depress salinities to near zero for several weeks at a time and which send concentrations of suspended sediment soaring to levels far too high for the oyster to handle. One bar off Tolchester in the upper Bay has been wiped out by floods at least eight times between 1900 and 1970, and once again during 1972 by Tropical Storm Agnes.

The oyster is bathed in a soup rich with food. To live, heshe pumps: pumps food and oxygen in, pumps wastes out. To feed, heshe acts like a submarine vacuum cleaner, obtaining food by filtering it from the surrounding waters. By beating the millions of cilia on heshe's gills, the oyster drives water through the gill slits. Fine particles caught by the hair-like cilia are wrapped in a sheath of mucus and passed along to the labial palps, the mouth, where they may be either ingested as food or rejected as pseudofeces. A microscopic examination of the gut of an oyster may reveal diatoms and other phytoplankton, zooplankton, larvae, pollen grains, silt particles, and bacteria; lots of bacteria.

The rate at which an oyster pumps is determined by the temperature and by other environmental conditions. At very low temperatures, below 35°F, oysters are sluggish and there is virtually no feeding. The same is true at relatively high temperatures, above 90°F. At both extremes the oyster is stressed, and there is little activity. Between these limits, the rate of pumping increases with temperature, the maximum being about 10 gallons per hour, a pumping rate

the oyster can sustain for several hours at a stretch. Over a 24-hour period, an adult oyster may filter as much as 100 gallons of Bay water, removing from it particles down to a few thousandths of an inch in size. What a wonderful vacuum cleaner.

The concentration of particles suspended within the water and other properties also determine the rate at which the oyster pumps and feeds. If too much sediment is stirred up from the bottom by tidal currents, surface waves, or baymen's tongs and dredges, the oyster may simply stop feeding and close. Or if the food is of a wrong kind, heshe may also close up.

Oysters grow well in salinities ranging from as low as 8 or 10‰ to that of full sea water, 34 to 35‰. They grow more rapidly in the upper third of this range, but so also do their worst predators: the oyster drill, the starfish, and the boring sponge—all deadly enemies. The same is true of MSX, a microscopic parasite that attacks oysters and which has caused massive mortalities. Because the oyster's enemies are not able to tolerate the lower salinities, the Bay's oyster population is concentrated in areas of relatively low salinity; those between 10 and 20‰. The oysters may grow more slowly there, but they have a better chance of surviving.

The Bay's good seed areas are not necessarily the best areas for "raising" the oysters to market size. Because the salinity, food supply, and other environmental conditions may be less desirable in the seed areas than they are in others, and to relieve overcrowding that can limit growth, young oysters are frequently dredged from the seed areas after a few months and replanted in good growing areas from which they will later be harvested. There are at present few self-sustaining natural oyster bars in the Bay. Many decades of over-fishing have robbed the Bay bottom of clean oyster shells to serve as hard substrate for setting. Without active programs to transplant cultch, old oyster shells that provide a firm bottom on which to set, and to transplant seed oysters themselves, it is unlikely that the Bay's oyster production could be sustained.

THE WATER FLEA
(Podon polyphemoides)

The water flea *(Podon polyphemoides)*, a tiny brachiopod crustacean, is one of the most abundant animals among the Bay's plankton. It is a relative of another, much better known, crustacean, *Callinectes sapidus*, the blue crab.

Each spring the hatching of overwintered eggs deposited in the soft sediments of the Bay's shallow tributaries, including the South, Chester, Magothy, Severn, and Miles rivers and Eastern Bay, initiates the annual cycle of planktonic *Podon*. In the early spring, when bottom water temperatures have warmed to about 40°F, water fleas by the billions, not larval forms but miniature adults each about one-hundredth of an inch long (one-fifth the size of the head of a pin), pop from the sediments and stream up through the water column toward the sunlit surface. Unlike its crustacean cousin the blue crab, *Podon* goes through no larval stage. Most of the newly hatched water fleas are asexual parthenogenetic females; females produced from unfertilized eggs. Each will produce a clutch of similar females, which will be released as small adults when the mother moults. Many of this brood of asexual females are already pregnant themselves even before they are released from the maternal brood sac. During the spring the tributaries literally swarm with water fleas, sometimes in excess of 50,000 to a single cubic yard of water.

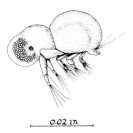

├── 0.02 in. ──┤

Podon polyphemoides
(water flea)

Within a month, *Podon* spread into the main body of the Bay. By mid-April populations in the tributaries have declined, and the water fleas are concentrated in a single continuous patch that stretches down the middle reaches of the Bay from north of the Severn to the mouth of the Potomac. Concentrations of *Podon* may reach 100,000 per cubic yard of water and may account for 95 percent of the volume of zooplankton in a sample. The population peaks rapidly by the first of May, declines during the summer, recovers slightly during the fall, and crashes as winter sets in. By the end of January water fleas have disappeared from the plankton. This cycle is repeated every year, year after year. Its success depends upon a curious combination of asexual and sexual activity. Asexual reproduction of unfertilized eggs is the principal way *Podon* reproduces in the Bay, but each spring and fall asexual females produce males and sexual females that mate to form sexual overwintering eggs. These will replenish the diminished population the following year. By producing overwintering eggs twice during the year *Podon* guards against catastrophic effects of environmental extremes and enhances the chances for the continued success of the species.

Podon preys, by preference, upon other animals and, when necessary, eats plants in the plankton. Truly a Polyphemus, it has a single well-developed movable compound eye—only one—to spot its prey, well-developed appendages to grasp it, and well-developed mandibles to chew and to rasp it. *Podon's* importance as a source of food for other organisms in the food web is not yet well established.

One of the puzzles set by the water flea is how the population manages to maintain itself for months on end as a well-defined bump in a fixed position within the Bay considering *Podon's* poor swimming ability. Why isn't it flushed out to sea or, at least, diffused over a wider area as are most passive materials? Since the greatest numbers of *Podon* are within the upper layer, at least during the daytime when most scientists are watching them, one would expect that the feebly swimming water fleas would be slowly swept down the Bay by the net motion of the upper layer, ultimately to be carried into the sea. But they are not.

Podon, like many other zooplankton, has found a way to use the machinery of the Bay to hold its position horizontally within the Bay. Even though it is not much of a swimmer, *Podon* can move up and down in the water column with relative ease. Early each morning water fleas in the Bay's landward flowing lower layer are stirred by the light of the rising sun filtering down through the murky waters of the Bay and respond by rising into the surface layer. They spend the morning and most of the afternoon near the surface feeding on other plankton. Each afternoon as the sun gets low in the sky they descend rapidly into the landward flowing lower layer where they spend the night. Next morning they move back up to the surface layer to feed and repeat the cycle. This vertical migration divides their time between the seaward flowing upper layer and the landward flowing lower layer. The only way *Podon* can hold position is to alternate between the two layers and to spend, on the average, more than half its time in the lower layer; but not too much or it will be carried too far upstream. In the Bay, the only way for a floater to go nowhere is to move up and down.

Many zooplankton migrate vertically like *Podon*, but most spend their nights near the surface and their days in the depths. Why *Podon* does it in reverse is an unsolved mystery.

THE BLUE CRAB
(Callinectes sapidus)

The blue crab (*Callinectes sapidus*) is a crustacean decapod, a hard-shelled animal with ten legs. The hindmost pair is modified into swimming paddles and the foremost into claws adapted for tearing and grinding. Like the striped bass and the oyster, it emerges from the egg as a larval form that joins the plankton. Unlike its cousin, *Podon*, it has a larval form. The adult striped bass is a strong swimmer. The adult oyster remains forever fixed to the bottom. The water flea is a floater. In contrast, the adult blue crab is a strong agile swimmer who spends long stretches buried in the bottom mud and scavenges for food near the bottom.

Summer, particularly August, is mating time for the blue crab. "Jimmies," sexually mature males and "sooks," sexually mature females, marked by a U-shaped telson on the underside rather than the V-shape of the immature, pair off in the middle reaches of the Bay. But impregnation is impossible until the female has shed the armor of her shell. The jimmies seem able to predict when a shed is imminent and, not to miss an opportunity, latch on to the sooks and carry them about with them cradled beneath their bodies. These are the so-called "doublers" since the jimmy releases his grip with the greatest reluctance and the pair can be dipped out together with a net.

The jimmy is a solicitous mate. Doubled, the male begins by searching out a protected spot, an eelgrass bed, an old rusty bucket, any secure and private hiding place. Once the female has shed her shell, she is a "soft crab" and helpless for two or three days. Impregnation takes six to twelve hours and the jimmy does not leave the sook after he has finished but continues to cradle her until her new shell has hardened and she is once again able to fend for herself. The jimmy, however, is not monogamous. After seeing his mate well on her way he is once more on the prowl. The sook, on the other hand, will never mate again.

The jimmy remains "on station" but, upon parting, the sook begins to work her way down the margins of the Bay toward the area near the Capes, which is the spawning ground of the blue crab. After sleeping-out the winter in the bottom mud, the sook will emerge to cast her fertile eggs, perhaps two million of them, only two of which, on the average, will survive to become adults.

The migrations of the jimmies are much shorter and do not bring them back to the spawning ground. Once a male has left the nursery, he never returns. This pattern sorts the sexes, separating the sexually mature females from the males. In the upper reaches of the Bay, one catches mostly jimmies; in the lower Bay, mostly "mollies," the generally popular name for female blue crabs.

As winter comes on the crabs disappear from the waters of the Bay. They slide off the shoals and down into the deep trough that marks the ancestral Susquehanna River Valley. The colder the winter, the deeper they go. For the jimmies, the waters off Smith Point near the mouth of the Potomac, where the water depths reach 100 feet or more, is a favorite spot. However, wintering jimmies line the entire middle reaches of the Bay extending as far north as Annapolis. The crabs back into the soft Bay sediment at a 45° angle, working their way in until only their antennae and eye stalks are left exposed and there they lie dormant, male and female, young and old, waiting for spring.

The sleep of crabs who have been fortunate enough to come to rest in Maryland waters, principally jimmies, will be unbroken. Maryland law forbids dredging for crabs. But those bedded down in Virginia waters, mainly sooks, cannot rest easy. Virginia permits winter dredging for crabs and, for the eastern seaboard, the Virginia catch alone makes up 60 percent of the entire winter harvest. Many sooks will be rudely awakened from their torpid state and wrenched from their sedimentary beds.

When spring comes and the locusts are in bloom, the crabs emerge from the bottom to resume active life in the water. The business of the sooks is then, perhaps, the most crucial for the continued well-being of the species.

In May the sook opens her abdomen and attaches her fertilized eggs to her telson where they form an orangish-yellow spongy mass. This gives her yet another popular name. She is now a "sponge crab" or "punk." The punks feed vigorously to nourish their increasingly massive and cumbersome egg masses, which by mid-June turn dark brown or black. Upon full ma-

turity, a flexure of the punk's abdomen showers millions of the first larval form of the blue crab, the zoeae, into the water to join the plankton where they swim feebly to the sunlit surface waters.

During the first six weeks of life, the zoeae moult several times, becoming increasingly complex structurally with each moult. At its final moult, the zoea takes the second larval form, megalops, which looks like a misbegotten lobster. Megalops is 0.06 to 0.12 inches long and is complete with claws and a tail. When it becomes a crab the tail will turn under against the abdomen to form the telson. Megalops is a stronger swimmer than zoea but it prefers to stay near the bottom. It is as megalops that the blue crab begins its trek up the Bay toward lower salinities, moulting and changing as it goes until it becomes, finally, a tiny but recognizable blue crab.

Moulting continues. The crab grows but its shell does not. When there is no room left the shell must be shed and replaced with a larger one. Thus, the crab's size increases by jerks. The young crabs, while small, shed every few days. As they become older and larger, shedding becomes more difficult, and 25 to 50 days may pass between the moults of a mature adult. Shedding is a physically exhausting business. A "soft crab," one which has lost its old shell and whose new shell is not yet hard, is exhausted with the struggle and utterly defense-

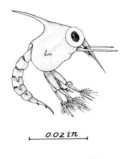

0.02 in.

Callinectes sapidus
(blue crab) zoea

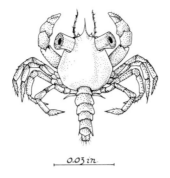

Callinectes sapidus
(blue crab) megalops

less. It has lost its protective exoskeleton. And, even worse, it can hardly move. Even if its muscles were not so limp and tired, they have no firm points of attachment and so no real leverage. A soft crab can't run for it; he can only try to hide until his new shell hardens.

By the summer or fall of the year following his appearance as a zoea, the crab is sexually mature, ready to make his contribution to the life cycle that sustains the species.

Near the end of the summer many of the old sooks who have spawned leave the Bay for the ocean to die. A few will live to return to the Bay during the following summer, but they will never again mate. They are easy to spot. Their bodies are studded with barnacles and their once brilliant colors dulled by sea moss. No blue crab, male or female, has a long life, three years at most, and much of it is spent sleeping; most of the rest in a search for food.

The blue crab is a coarse feeder—a scavenger. Not to put too fine a point on it, the blue crab prefers dead garbage; the higher, the better. In this he plays an important role among the recyclers by tearing up and eating the larger hunks of rotting organic matter. This makes it easier for the smaller recyclers, including the bacteria, to complete the work. The blue crab is an important member of the Bay's sanitation crew.

The chemical and physical conditions in the Bay at the time zoeae are released play an im-

portant part in the success of the blue crab. A high river flow that depresses salinities below 25‰ will be followed by massive mortalities. It will also increase the risk that those left alive will be flushed out to sea. They may also be flushed out by another mechanism. Prolonged strong winds blowing up the Bay force excess water into the Bay from the continental shelf and keep it there. When the winds die out, the system relaxes and this tremendous mass of water rushes back to the sea. The discharge to the sea through the Virginia Capes may exceed the average discharge by more than ten-fold. Flows may be so great that they completely overpower the tidal currents for two days or more. In its rush to purge itself of all this unwanted water, the Bay also expels anything suspended in it, including crab larvae. Larvae by the billions may be swept out to sea, many of them permanently lost to the Bay.

BIOLOGICAL SIGNALS OF POTENTIAL BAY PROBLEMS

We have taken a brief look, a peek, at the life cycles of four of the Bay's animals. Only four kinds of animals out of thousands, but the successes and failures of these four can give us clues about others, and can alert us, perhaps, to potential problems resulting from society's uses of this great estuarine system.

There are large year-to-year variations in the success of each new year-class of striped bass. These may be due to natural factors, to human impacts, or to both. Which and what we do not really know. The Chesapeake Bay, which is believed to produce more striped bass than all the rest of North America combined, has not had a strong year class since 1970. The females still produce eggs by the billions; the males still fertilize them. But something is amiss. The eggs develop only partially and, after a certain stage is reached, suffer massive mortalities. Some have ascribed this failure to persistent additions of low levels of chlorinated hydrocarbons discharged into the Bay by industry and sewage treatment plants; both point sources. Others feel that the trouble comes from the chlorinated hydrocarbons used in herbicides and pesticides and drained from agricultural land; non-point sources. The striped bass presents us with a problem to which we have, as yet, no solution.

The success of the oyster depends upon the natural biological, chemical, geological, and physical processes that characterize the Bay, and upon man; not only upon the watermen who harvest the oyster, but upon people and their activities throughout the Bay's drainage basin. Until 1980, there had been no significant recruitment of new oysters for a decade, except in local areas in Eastern Bay, in the Choptank River, the lower Potomac River, and in upper Tangier Sound. Most oysters in the Bay today are old and large. The reasons are obscure. There is good reason for concern about the oyster in Chesapeake Bay.

Of the four animals we have considered, *Podon* is the most stable; its population most uniform from year to year; its cycles most predictable, *Podon*'s modes and patterns of reproduction mitigate against the vagaries of nature and society.

Just as for the striped bass and the oyster, the success of the blue crab is highly variable, and the causal factors remain largely unexplained. Some years are good and catchable crabs are fat and plentiful. Other years it seems, to watermen, at least, that there are hardly any. My impression is that for watermen, good years for crabs are like the Red Queen's "Jam every other day." For them, it never seems to come up good crabbing this year. But the landing data tell another story. Commercial landings do fluctuate widely. For a 20-year period from 1954 to 1973 they ranged from a low of 22,000 tons in 1955 to a high of 48,000 tons in 1966, but there is no apparent long-term trend of either a decline or an increase in commercial harvest. Still it bears close watching.

In a system as dynamic as the Chesapeake Bay, the large natural fluctuations in environmental properties affect the life cycles of its inhabitants and produce large variations in their successes and abundances. Superimposed upon these are the effects of people; the effects of pollution and overfishing, of channel dredging for navigation and winter dredging for crabs, of power plant entrainment, and of the filling and draining of wetlands. Because the natural fluctuations are so large and our data base so limited, it is exceedingly difficult to isolate the effects of people from those of nature. But if we wait until society's "signals" can be separated from nature's "noise," it may well be too late for effective planning and management.

As our friend the Walrus said, "The time has come . . . to talk of many things . . ."

Planning for the Bay

Our plans miscarry because we have no aim. When a man does not know what harbor he is making for, no wind is the right wind.
—Seneca

We have had the Chesapeake Bay, or one of its ancestors, for as long as human beings have been in the region. They grew up with it. They accompanied it as it moved across the continental shelf and into its present basin. They saw it grow and expand from a small embayment confined to a narrow valley of the Susquehanna near the outer edge of the continental shelf 15,000 years ago into a vast inland sea. The Bay has always been vital to the people who have clustered around its shores. As the ages have rolled on, the life of mankind has become vastly more complicated than it was 15,000 years ago, 10,000 years ago, 2,000 years ago, or even 200 years ago. So, too, has the life of the Bay. The demands on it are greater—greater in variety and in intensity.

We have seen that on a geological time scale the Bay is only an ephemeral feature; that it will last at most another 10,000, perhaps 20,000, years if sea level remains steady; less if sea level falls; more if it rises. While what people do to the Bay pales into insignificance in comparison with the effects of the major swings in sea level associated with glaciations and deglaciations, their influence is nevertheless profound. Measured on time scales of decades or centuries, human activities even dominate some aspects, among them most particularly water quality and the diversity and abundance of the organisms that inhabit the Bay. It is with these compressed time scales that we must concern ourselves if we are to manage the Bay. To discuss estuaries on geological time scales may be philosophically satisfying and appropriate when we turn our attention to their ephemeral nature and to their importance for the evolution and survival of the species, but geological time scales can not satisfy us when we come to assess their importance to people and to society. The time scale we use must fit the nature of the problem we examine. One can hardly use a sun dial to time a hundred-yard dash.

The span the Bay will occupy in the geologic record will be determined primarily by climatic events, but poor soil conservation throughout its drainage basin could easily cut its geological lifetime in half. But there are more urgent reasons for sound management of the Bay than a simple desire to extend its geological lifetime. Without effective management, the biologically and recreationally useful life of the Bay might well be only one-tenth of its geological life. Such negligent shortening of the Bay's useful life would not mean extinction for the estuarine-dependent species of shellfish and finfish that use it. They have survived the destruction of many "Bays." But the concentrations of organisms within the Bay might drop so low that they could not be effectively and efficiently harvested. The fisheries, which are a human activity and a human good, would vanish. We would be the loser. Of all the organisms in the biosphere, man is clearly the most estuarine-dependent.

We use the Bay as a supplier of extractable resources, organic and inorganic; as a transient receiver for industrial and human wastes; as a source of industrial process water; as a source of cooling water for power plants; as an avenue for shipping and transportation; as a military training ground for testing ordnance; and as a recreational—a re-creational—resource. All of these uses are probably "legitimate." Few, if any, are so damaging that they should be prohibited out of hand and, if the intensity of a use remains below some threshold, it need not even be seriously restrictive. Trouble arises because the demands made on the Bay are sometimes in conflict and because the limiting thresholds are difficult to define. Conflict arises mainly between such activities as fisheries and recreation, which require a certain level of environmental quality, and activities for which quality is unimportant, activities which, in fact, frequently lead to a degradation of environmental quality. There is also a conflict between military and civilian uses of the Bay, because large areas are set aside for ordnance testing and for training. Civilian activities are restricted by military regulation in about 17 percent of the Chesapeake Bay estuarine system. This is nearly twice the total area of the shellfish bars closed because of high coliform bacteria counts.

The greatest threat by far to the biologically and aesthetically useful life span of the Bay comes from pollution. A pollutant is any substance that causes pollution. That much is incontrovertible. There are, however, two ways to define pollution. One can define pollution as any unnatural addition to the environment regardless of whether it has adverse effects or not. Or, one can restrict the term pollution to those unnatural additions that result in demonstrably deleterious effects. The dictionary defines "to pollute" as "to make foul or unclean, to taint, to defile, or to soil." Thus, the word clearly implies a value judgment: pollution *per se* is "bad." If we accept this view, we should use the second definition: pollution is any unnatural addition to the environment that reduces its utility.

The point at which a substance causes pollution, the point at which it becomes a pollutant, depends not only on the substance itself but on its effect on the environment into which it is introduced; and that depends on the concentration of the substance in the environment. Thus, if we call a material a potential pollutant, we mean that under some circumstances it could cause pollution. The presence of a potential pollutant does not necessarily mean that there is pollution. At low concentrations, the presence of a potential pollutant may actually improve the environment. Copper, for example, is necessary for phytoplankton growth and reproduction, but too much copper is toxic. Nutrients are essential for primary productivity, but they, too, can become pollutants when they are too plentiful or of the wrong form. Heavy metals, chlorinated hydrocarbons (PCBs), pesticides, herbicides, oil, heat, chlorine, sediment, even salt water and fresh water are all potential pollutants. Most substances are. But some among them, the anthropogenic substances, such as chlorinated hydrocarbons (PCBs and Kepone, for example), are clearly more menacing than the others and have no known environmental benefits at any level of concentration. The difficulty is that we rarely know how closely we are approaching the Bay's assimilative capacity for any of these potential pollutants: its capacity to receive them individually and collectively before they threaten the ecology of the Bay. We are, in effect, continually titrating the Bay against the input of hundreds, perhaps thousands, of contaminants, but unfortunately we do not know what indicators will tell us how closely we are approaching their endpoints. Only after we over-shoot the limit do we realize that we have gone too far.

We should identify the documented and potential sources of contaminants; delimit the locations and the strengths of these sources—both the point sources such as pipe discharges and the non-point sources such as the general seepage of pesticides from farm lands; assess their impacts on the environment and the biota; and establish limiting concentrations in the water, in the sediments, and in a variety of representative organisms to ensure adequate protection of the resources and the uses of the Bay that we wish to conserve. This is a large undertaking, but we must do it if we are ever to develop an effective management program for the Bay. It is a job we should have started yesterday. Today is none too soon to begin. And it must be continued without remission if we are ever to manage the Bay in any real sense.

Appropriate management of the Bay would balance the demands on the Bay in some sensible way to minimize conflicts within the Bay and within the society that depends too heavily upon it. This is a difficult task; one that has not yet been done satisfactorily. It requires not only that we "Save the Bay" but also that we know what we are saving it for. Sophisticated strategies must be devised to achieve predetermined ends.

One way to improve our effectiveness in managing the Bay would be to zone it into segments within which different water "quality" standards and criteria would apply. For each segment these standards and criteria would have to be consistent with the natural processes prevailing in them and with the uses perceived to be most important for that segment. At present, formal zoning of the Bay is limited largely to military activities and major shipping channels. But the zoning concept has been well proven. We zone our terrestrial environment into residential and industrial areas, we set aside portions of it for parks and forests, and we reserve segments of it for the disposal of our wastes. We do not make it official policy to spread our garbage and trash uniformly over the landscape. We neither demand nor expect all parts of our terrestrial environment to be of equal "quality."

Segments of the Bay could be designated as dredged material disposal areas, as receiving waters for municipal and industrial wastes, as sinks for heated effluents from electric generating plants, as spawning and nursery areas, as military testing areas, and as fishing and recreational areas. Still others could be preserved, or at least conserved, in a "wild" state. These designations are not necessarily exclusive. Some uses are compatible. Some zones might even receive seasonal designations. The identification of a finfish spawning area certainly would not preclude its use as a recreational area for people. If we accept the view that the primary reasons for managing the Bay are to protect its biological resources and to conserve its recreational and aesthetic values for human use, then certain activities should be restricted more severely in some areas than in others and also at some times than at others. For example, greater restriction would apply during those periods when organisms are most vulnerable, presumably during the egg and larval stages of commercially and recreationally important species of finfish and shellfish.

In one sense, zoning the Bay would be more difficult than zoning the terrestrial environment that surrounds it. The medium—water—is more reactive and more mobile than the land. However, once the desired uses of a Bay segment have been selected, implementation should be simpler since, in general, the water and most of the bottom are publicly owned. The objective for the Bay, however, is essentially the same as it is for the land.

Zoning is a formal restriction on use and constitutes a police power. The primary purpose of zoning is to manage. But manage for what? . . . for whom? Management must be directed at some goal or goals if it is to be effective. Good managers, like good scientists, must set significant but realistic goals—goals that, once reached, will produce worthwhile and desired results— and, further, goals that have a reasonable probability of being attainable as well. Environmental management is an exercise in decision theory, and the stakes are too high to be left to any one special interest group, or even to several. Before any zoning plan can be established, priorities must be assigned to the uses of the specific areas under consideration. This is the most difficult task in any zoning. In terms of gross monetary return the "most important" uses of the Bay are for shipping and transportation, industry, and military activities. The monetary values of commercial fisheries and of recreational activities are also very great, although more difficult to assess. And if communion with nature is indeed one of man's ultimate sources of happiness, as I, for one, firmly believe, then the recreational and aesthetic values of the Bay are extremely high even though they may not be measured in dollars and cents. The establishment of priorities clearly involves not only the economy but also the environment, and even society as a whole. Management problems rarely have unequivocal solutions. They almost always require value judgments. Natural scientists have no particular qualifications for making such decisions. At best, they can solve only a few of people's simpler problems. Indeed, from time to time, their solutions have inadvertently created problems. Science cannot determine incontestably either what uses of the Bay are most important, or even what uses are most desirable. Through science we can learn to understand how the Bay works and in part even how to control it, but science cannot decisively determine the ways in which we should control it and use it. Scientists, on the other hand, can help to design the strategies and to implement the actions necessary to reach desired ends once they have been identified. They can also help assess whether intended uses and ends are attainable, or how closely they can be approached, and at what costs to the environment. They can evaluate the environmental effects of alternatives far better than any other group of individuals. This is the role they can play.

Effective estuarine zoning must take into account not only present and potential uses of each segment, but existing and desirable uses of the contiguous coast. One could, for example, prohibit sewer outfalls in a segment by zoning the receiving waters, but such action would have little effect on water "quality" if there were large adjacent distributed sources from agricultural runoff or septic field drainage.

A zoning plan would not be a substitute for proper sewage treatment, for effective dredging and dredged material management, for thoughtful siting and operation of power plants, for stringent criteria and standards to protect the environment and the biota, and for marked reduction in the inputs of toxic wastes. It would be a tool to make these efforts and programs more effective in conserving multiple uses of the Bay, the very thing that makes it so priceless.

Nature and history have already done much of the zoning for us. The major finfish spawning and nursery areas are set; they are a function of salinity and habitat and could not be shifted without great expense—and perhaps not at all. Our most important and expansive salt marshes are already in place; others could be constructed but they could not begin to compare with Blackwater and the Bay's other great marshes. So, too, are some of the major industrial activities firmly entrenched.

The Port of Baltimore lies at the head of the Patapsco estuary in the upper Chesapeake Bay. To relocate it or shut it down is unthinkable. The economy of the entire State of Maryland would be seriously disrupted. If one were starting out today with a *tabula rasa,* a clean slate, to site industrial activities, one might well choose not to locate a major port in Baltimore. The prevailing depths in the Patapsco estuary and on its approaches are considerably less than the depths required by even medium-sized ocean-going vessels, and the high sedimentation rates make maintenance dredging a necessity. Furthermore, because the Baltimore harbor is in the upper reaches of the Chesapeake Bay, ships must travel relatively long distances within the Bay through important shellfish, finfish, and recreational areas to enter it. With every passage there is the risk of collision and an accidental release of materials into the Bay. Despite these drawbacks, the Port of Baltimore *is* at the head of the Patapsco in the upper reaches of the Chesapeake Bay, and it will neither move nor go out of business. Fortunately, there is no reason to believe that the operation of a viable Port of Baltimore is incompatible with a healthy Bay. Proper regional planning is the key.

The Bay as a whole is still in relatively good shape, not because of people, but in spite of them. It is not too late to conserve this precious resource. Fortunately, the Bay and other estuaries are not as fragile as some would have us believe. They are among the most resilient ecosystems on Earth; their inhabitants are well tuned to dramatic changes, able to endure substantial environmental insults from nature or man, and still recover. But the Bay's tolerance is not infinite. We can exceed its elastic limit—its ability to bounce back without permanent damage to the characteristics we prize. The stresses and strains that face the Bay today are far greater and more complex than they have ever been. The potential damage is far more menacing; the potential recovery times far longer. This is the time for decisive environmental action; before there is a crisis; while the Bay is still a relatively healthy patient, one that can respond to therapy. The time is now.

We should identify the uses of the Bay we want to conserve and the characteristics of the Bay on which those uses depend and then go on to develop effective management strategies to sustain them. We should content ourselves only with predictable and acceptable risks to the Bay's milieu and its biota. The Bay cannot be preserved but, with care and thoughtful planning, it can be conserved. This is what we should strive for; what we should plan for. Planning is people-centered, people-oriented. This is as it should be. The Bay's problems are humanity's problems: too many people, too many uses. We are only one of innumerable organisms that use the Bay, but our effects are pervasive. Our demands are more varied and more complex than are those of any other organism. And they are frequently in conflict—in conflict among themselves and in conflict with uses of other organisms. Of all the organisms that use the Bay, only man can destroy it for all the others. Being the only rational animal, he is also the only one who can plan for its future. We are, indeed, the Bay's keeper.

Photographs

OF THE LIVING CHESAPEAKE

Striped bass fishermen, Upper Bay, ca. 1970.

Fishermen, Upper Bay, ca. 1968.

Hand-tonging for oysters, Upper Bay, ca. 1970.

Patent-tonging for oysters, Upper Bay, ca. 1970.

Susquehanna Flats, ca. 1970.

Back Creek, Maryland, ca. 1966.

Skipjacks, Choptank Estuary, ca. 1972.

Skipjack, 1974.

Skipjack transplanting shells below Bay Bridge at Annapolis, ca. 1967.

Squall, Lower Bay, 1969.

Patent-tonging for oysters, Upper Bay, 1971.

Patent-tonging for oysters, Upper Bay, 1972.

Striped bass fishermen, ca. 1968.

Skipjack, ca. 1966.

Derelict skipjack, Eastern Shore, ca. 1970.

Eastern Shore, ca. 1970.

Derelict boats, Eastern Shore, ca. 1968.

Rappahannock River, ca. 1965.

Baltimore Harbor, ca. 1972.

Blackwater National Wildlife Refuge, 1968.

Abandoned pier, Baltimore Harbor, 1970.

Blackwater National Wildlife Refuge, 1973.

Blackwater National Wildlife Refuge, 1973.

Skipjack running for cover, ca. 1972.

Winter at Blackwater Marsh, 1972.

Upper Bay, 1971.

Shore ice, 1966.

Patent-tonging for oysters off Annapolis, 1974.

Smith Island, 1970.

Canada geese, Choptank River Estuary, 1973.

Conowingo Reservoir, ca. 1965.

Lower Chesapeake Bay, 1972.

James River, 1967.

Early morning, Annapolis, ca. 1970.

Flag Ponds, Maryland, 1964.

Derelict boat, Eastern Shore, 1967.

Tolchester Beach, ca. 1964.

Striped bass fishermen, Upper Bay, ca. 1968.

Susquehanna River shad, 1968.

Patent-tonging for oysters, Upper Bay, ca. 1970.

Patent-tonging for oysters, Chester River Estuary, ca. 1970.

Skipjacks, Choptank Estuary, ca. 1970.

Clouds, Lower Bay, 1971.

Skipjacks off Kent Island, 1972.

Worton Creek, 1963.

Seagull, 1974.

Skipjack, ca. 1966.

Deal Island, ca. 1968.

Derelict boat, Eastern Shore, 1964.

Eastern Shore, ca. 1970.

Fisherman's shanty, 1970.

Tolchester Beach, ca. 1964.

Buyboat, Annapolis, ca. 1964.

Blackwater National Wildlife Refuge, 1969.

Hand-tonging for oysters, Chester River Estuary, ca. 1969.

Early morning, Annapolis, ca. 1970.

Setting stakes for gill nets, Upper Bay, 1965.

Fisherman, Havre de Grace, ca. 1968.

Gill net fisherman, Upper Bay, ca. 1968.

Derelict boat, Eastern Shore, 1968.

Grove Point, Upper Bay, 1966.

Blackwater National Wildlife Refuge, 1970.

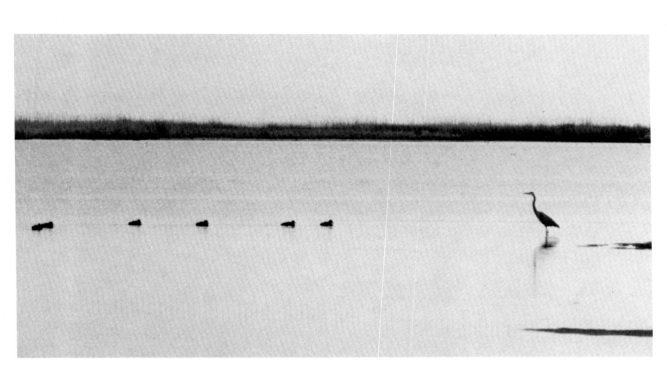

Eastern Neck Wildlife Refuge, ca. 1972.

Blackwater National Wildlife Refuge, 1972.

Blackwater National Wildlife Refuge, ca. 1973.

Striped bass fishermen, Upper Bay, ca. 1968.

Fishermen, Upper Bay, ca. 1966.

Storm clouds, Eastern Bay, 1972.

Skipjack, 1972.

J. R. SCHUBEL has been Director of the State University of New York's Marine Sciences Research Center since 1974. Before that, he spent fourteen years with The Johns Hopkins University's Chesapeake Bay Institute, first as a graduate student, then as a staff member. When he left in 1974 he was a Research Scientist, Adjunct Research Professor, and Associate Director. He received his Ph.D. from The Johns Hopkins University in 1968, has published over one hundred articles, and has edited several books on estuarine and coastal oceanography.